Palgrave Studies in Cybercrime and Cybersecurity

Series Editors:

Marie-Helen Maras
John Jay College of Criminal Justice CUN
New York, USA

Thomas J. Holt
Michigan State University
East Lansing, Michigan, USA

Aim of the Series:
This book series addresses the urgent need to advance knowledge in the fields of cybercrime and cybersecurity. Because the exponential expansion of computer technologies and use of the Internet have greatly increased the access by criminals to people, institutions, and businesses around the globe, the series will be international in scope. It provides a home for cutting-edge long-form research. Further, the series seeks to spur conversation about how traditional criminological theories apply to the online environment. The series welcomes contributions from early career researchers as well as established scholars on a range of topics in the cybercrime and cybersecurity fields.

More information about this series at
http://www.springer.com/series/14637

Thomas J. Holt • Olga Smirnova • Yi-Ting Chua

Data Thieves in Action

Examining the International Market for Stolen Personal Information

Thomas J. Holt
Michigan State University
East Lansing, Michigan, USA

Olga Smirnova
East Carolina University
Greenville, USA

Yi-Ting Chua
Michigan State University
East Lansing, USA

Palgrave Studies in Cybercrime and Cybersecurity
ISBN 978-1-137-58903-3   ISBN 978-1-137-58904-0   (eBook)
DOI 10.1057/978-1-137-58904-0

Library of Congress Control Number: 2016950639

© The Editor(s) (if applicable) and The Author(s) 2016
This work is subject to copyright. All rights are solely and exclusively licensed by the Publisher, whether the whole or part of the material is concerned, specifically the rights of translation, reprinting, reuse of illustrations, recitation, broadcasting, reproduction on microfilms or in any other physical way, and transmission or information storage and retrieval, electronic adaptation, computer software, or by similar or dissimilar methodology now known or hereafter developed.
The use of general descriptive names, registered names, trademarks, service marks, etc. in this publication does not imply, even in the absence of a specific statement, that such names are exempt from the relevant protective laws and regulations and therefore free for general use.
The publisher, the authors and the editors are safe to assume that the advice and information in this book are believed to be true and accurate at the date of publication. Neither the publisher nor the authors or the editors give a warranty, express or implied, with respect to the material contained herein or for any errors or omissions that may have been made.

Cover illustration: Modern building window © saulgranda/Getty

Printed on acid-free paper

This Palgrave Macmillan imprint is published by Springer Nature
The registered company is Nature America Inc. New York

Tom Holt: This work is dedicated to my beautiful wife and daughters
Olga Smirnova: To my incredible husband, Steve; my parents, Olga, Sasha,
and Victor; and my in-laws, Tony and Gloria
Yi-Ting Chua: To my wonderful family and friends

Acknowledgments

We are grateful to the many individuals whose assistance and contributions to the development of this work facilitated its creation, value, and applicability. First, we must thank the National Institute of Justice, Office of Justice Programs, US Department of Justice, who sponsored this work under Grant No. 2010-IJ-CX-1676. The opinions, findings, and conclusions or recommendations expressed in this publication are those of the authors and do not reflect those of the Department of Justice. We would also like to thank the publishing team at Palgrave for their support and assistance throughout the creation and submission of this manuscript. Finally, we would like to thank our family and friends for all of their support throughout this process. The time spent during the holidays and breaks working on this text were challenging, and we appreciate their patience, love, and concern.

Contents

1 Introduction   1

2 The Marketing and Sales of Stolen Data   19

3 The Economic Impact of Stolen Data Markets   45

4 The Social Organization of Actors in Stolen Data Markets   73

5 Visualizing The Networks of Economic Transactions and Ads in Stolen Data Markets   97

6 Implications and Conclusions   133

Index   155

CHAPTER 1

Introduction

Abstract This chapter introduces the problem of stolen data markets as a consequence of the digital economy that now dominates society. Prior research studies on stolen data markets are discussed, along with their overlap with other electronic illicit markets like the Silk Road. The data for this book is described in detail. The focus is on a sample of threads from 13 forums operating around the world whose users communicate in Russian and English languages. The structure of the book is also elaborated chapter by chapter.

Keywords Data markets • Cybercrime • Identity fraud • Forums

In December 2013, the US retail giant Target announced that their in-store payment systems had been compromised by hackers. They did not immediately announce how much data had been lost, only that the compromise lasted between November 27 and December 15 and that customers' names, card number, expiration date, and CVV or card verification value were acquired (Target, 2014). Later that month, it was revealed that the breach may have affected 70 million people who shopped at stores across the country. The incident was rather shocking, particularly as it appeared to have been enabled by a weakness in the point of sale terminals, or cash register systems, in the stores themselves (Higgins, 2014). As a result, Target scrambled to respond to customer fears and provided detailed information on how individual victims could protect themselves in the event that their personal information was affected.

Though this story was shocking for many consumers who had not experienced such an incident before, it was just one of many large-scale data breaches that occurred over the last decade in the USA. In 2009, Heartland Payment Systems announced that their system security had been compromised during 2008 by a small group of hackers. The company processes over 11 million credit and debit card transactions a day for over 250,000 businesses across the USA. The impact of the breach was massive, as hackers were able to acquire information from 130 million credit and debit cards processed by 100,000 businesses (Verini, 2010). This was the largest breach of customer data in the USA, and was thought to stem from malicious software planted inside of the company's network in order to record payment data as it was sent by retail clients (Krebs, 2011). Even more disconcerting, this breach was apparently masterminded by Albert Gonzales and a few other hackers who compromised the payment systems of Marshalls department stores and its parent company, TJX, a few years prior. That compromise led to the loss of 45 million credit card records and over $1 billion in customer damages (Roberts, 2007). Thus, these actors were not simply hackers who were lucky enough to make one big score. Instead, they are proficient and dedicated repeat offenders who sought out high-value targets in succession and made lucrative profits as a result of their efforts.

The scope of these breaches demonstrates the substantial capacity of cybercriminals to acquire information in volumes far exceeding that of any successful street criminal. It is important to note that data breaches are not the only way in which personal information may be acquired in the digital age. As many as 51% of all adults in the USA use the Internet to engage in banking transactions, whether to check their balance or pay bills electronically (Fox, 2013), and 21% of adults use their mobile phone to engage in bank transactions through applications or the web (Federal Reserve, 2013). As a result, cybercriminals have found ways to exploit this process and surreptitiously access personal and financial information over the Internet (James, 2005; Newman & Clarke, 2003).

Dealing in Dumps: The Market for Stolen Data

In light of the growing prominence of electronic data theft and the significant financial harm that it may cause for individual victims and compromised companies, it is critical to consider what offenders do with the tremendous quantity of information that they obtain. There is no way that one person, or even a group of 10–20 people, could use hundreds of thousands of credit or debit cards in a short period of time. Even with the ability to make on-line purchases or transfer funds from victim accounts, there is simply too much information for any one individual to use it in a reasonable time frame.

As a consequence, there is now a burgeoning market for individuals to dispose of data that they obtain through data breaches and other forms of theft to others through web forums and Internet Relay Chat (IRC) channels (Chu, Holt, & Ahn, 2010; Dhanjani & Rios, 2008; Franklin, Paxson, Perrig, & Savage, 2007; Herley & Florencio, 2010; Holt & Lampke, 2010; Holz, Engelberth, & Freling, 2009; Honeynet Research Alliance, 2003; Motoyama, McCoy, Levchenko, Savage, & Voelker, 2011; Thomas & Martin, 2006; Wehinger, 2011). Though these markets are hosted in various countries around the world, many of the most active appear to operate out of Russia and Eastern Europe (Holt, 2013; Peretti, 2009; Symantec, 2012). Regardless of the location, the sales process begins when a seller posts an advertisement for a product or service, including their preferred mode of contact and payment method (Franklin et al., 2007; Holt & Lampke, 2010; Motoyama et al., 2011).

Typically, sellers accept on-line payments through various mechanisms depending on the market, including PayPal, PaySafeCards (Motoyama et al., 2011), e-Gold, Web Money (Franklin et al., 2007; Holt & Lampke, 2010), and other on-line systems. Real-world payments are also accepted by some sellers, though they must commonly be made through MoneyGram or Western Union, established services for the transfer of hard currency transnationally (Holt & Lampke, 2010; Motoyama et al., 2011). Interested buyers contact the seller and negotiate prices and complete transactions outside of the IRC channel or forum, typically through private messaging systems, ICQ, or email in order to help minimize their culpability or overt involvement in criminal exchanges (Franklin et al., 2007; Holt & Lampke, 2010; Motoyama et al., 2011). Though the hidden nature of market exchanges makes it difficult to document the quantity of materials sold, there is substantive research detailing the range of products offered by vendors. These markets primarily facilitate the sale of credit card and bank account information, personal identification numbers (PINs), and supporting customer information obtained through various forms of electronic fraud or theft in batches of tens or hundreds of accounts (Chu et al., 2010; Franklin et al., 2007; Holt & Lampke, 2010; Honeynet Research Alliance, 2003; Thomas & Martin, 2006). Although financial service providers from around the world are compromised, the bulk of stolen data sold in these markets appears to come from the USA, followed by various European nations (Franklin et al., 2007; Holt & Lampke, 2010).

In addition, these markets provide a venue for criminal service providers who offer resources to use illegally acquired information to obtain cash and products. For instance, individuals offer so-called cash-out services, where they may make transfers either from bank accounts to electronic accounts set up by a criminal, or through direct withdrawals at automatic teller machines (ATMs) in the real world all using stolen card data (Chu et al., 2010; Franklin et al., 2007; Holt & Lampke, 2010; Honeynet Research Alliance, 2003; Wehinger, 2011). Some will also operate "drops services" that will receive goods at residences in the real world that were purchased through on-line retailers using stolen card data, and fence or pawn the item to obtain hard currency (Holt & Lampke, 2010). Finally, a proportion of service providers specialize in the acquisition and sale of identity documents, such as passports and drivers licenses, to enable fraud and identity theft on- and off-line (Chu et al., 2010; Franklin et al., 2007; Holt & Lampke, 2010; Honeynet Research Alliance, 2003; Wehinger, 2011). Thus, the market for stolen data appears to be robust and diverse, providing a way to engage in cybercrimes without the need for interaction with any victim in the real world.

While a range of services are made available in these markets, the process of purchasing information is consistently structured from transaction to transaction as virtually all sellers require prospective buyers send payments first and will then deliver information or services to order (Franklin et al., 2007; Herley & Florencio, 2010; Holt & Lampke, 2010; Motoyama et al., 2011; Wehinger, 2011). The structure of the market favors sellers, as they have the desired information and the ability to dictate when and how it will be received. As a result, a number of enterprising players have entered markets in order to cheat or "rip off" customers by accepting payments, and then either by sending invalid accounts and false information or by simply not providing anything in return (Herley & Florencio, 2010; Holt & Lampke, 2010; Motoyama et al., 2011; Wehinger, 2011). There are no formal dispute resolution mechanisms that can be used by actors within the markets due to the illegal nature of their transactions (Holt & Lampke, 2010; Wehinger, 2011), thus making stolen data markets an excellent venue for predatory actors to generate substantial profits from naive buyers.

To minimize the risk of harm, some forums provide informal mechanisms that encourage trust between participants and sanction less reputable actors

(Holt, 2013; Holt & Lampke, 2010; Wehinger, 2011). Many markets allow buyers to publicly post feedback on their experience with a vendor in order to establish the credibility of a seller (Holt & Lampke, 2010; Motoyama et al., 2011; Wehinger, 2011). Since transactions occur outside of the forum, the ability to provide positive comments about a seller and their services appears to increase their potential share of the market, while those with negative feedback may eventually be ostracized and driven out of the community (Holt, 2013; Holt & Lampke, 2010; Motoyama et al., 2011).

A number of forums also provide mechanisms to insulate buyers and sellers from risk, such as the use of escrow payment systems (Holt, 2013; Holt & Lampke, 2010; Wehinger, 2011). A trusted party designated by the forum serves as an intermediary, or escrow agent, in the event both parties agree to use their services. If so, the escrow agent holds payments on behalf of a seller until the buyer confirms they have received the items they ordered (Holt, 2013; Holt & Lampke, 2010; Wehinger, 2011). The use of escrow payments allows a seller to establish their reputation and demonstrate they can be trusted, though it adds to the complexity of any transaction and is only an optional service offered by more established markets (Wehinger, 2011). In addition, administrators in both IRC channels and forums may ban sellers who scam or "rip off" customers by taking payments without delivering product (Holt & Lampke, 2010; Motoyama et al., 2011; Wehinger, 2011).

Sellers offer customer service mechanisms designed to attract customers and maintain a client base over time, through the use of bulk discounts, samples, and real-time customer support via various instant messaging (IM) clients (Franklin et al., 2007; Holt & Lampke, 2010; Wehinger, 2011). There is also some evidence that sellers in IRC channels post personal data, such as account numbers and victim names, which researchers argue is an attempt to demonstrate the validity of their products, or be viewed as a free sample (Dhanjani & Rios, 2008; Franklin et al., 2007; Holz et al., 2009; Symantec, 2008).

SITUATING THE MARKET FOR DATA IN THE LARGER ON-LINE ILLICIT ECONOMY

The development of stolen data markets may appear novel, though it is actually one part of a larger illicit economy operating on-line. There are a range of forums, websites, and content hosted on open parts of the Internet (see Holt & Bossler, 2016), as well as encrypted networks engaged in the sale of various products and services involving both virtual and real commodities (e.g. Martin, 2014). For instance, there are a number of forums and shops operating where hackers sell malicious software and cybercrime as a service to interested parties (e.g. Chu et al., 2010; Holt, 2013; Karami & McCoy, 2013; Li & Chen, 2014; Motoyama et al., 2011; Provos, Mavrommatis, Rajab, & Monroe, 2008). These markets enable individuals to buy new forms of malicious software, or lease existing infrastructure established through botnets and other malware platforms to engage in spamming, carding, and other forms of theft and fraud.

In much the same way, the Internet has revolutionized the sale of illegal products and services that can only be used in the real world. For example, prostitutes and their customers now utilize webpages and email as a means to advertise their services, arrange meetings, accept payments, and even validate their clients' identities prior to an encounter (e.g. Cunningham & Kendall, 2010; Holt & Blevins, 2007; Sanders, 2008). Even traditional marketplaces for on-line commerce like Craigslist play a role in the process of marketing sexual services directly to the general public (Cunningham & Kendall, 2010). As a result, the illicit sex trade has begun to move behind closed doors by reducing the need for some sex workers and customers to operate in street-based public advertising (Cunningham & Kendall, 2010; Quinn & Forsyth, 2013).

The sale of illicit drugs, ranging from prescription medications to hard drugs like cocaine, has also moved to on-line market places hosted through various mechanisms internationally (Martin, 2014). The majority of these markets are advertised in forums and web sites operating on the encrypted Tor network, which uses specialized software and browser protocols to hide the location of the site and the individuals connecting in. The use of Tor also allows individuals to create and host content through encrypted websites, minimizing the likelihood of law enforcement identification. To further conceal the identities of participants, individuals typically accept payment for products through on-line systems called crypto-currencies, meaning that the transaction is delivered through various encryption protocols that conceal the identity of the payer and the payee (Franklin, 2013; Martin, 2014).

In fact the development of cryptomarkets for drugs has drawn substantial attention from law enforcement, the media, and researchers (Franklin, 2013; Martin, 2014). One of the most famous of these markets was called the Silk Road, which began in 2011 to enable individuals to buy various materials ranging from computer equipment to clothing, though a subsection of the market offering narcotics and manufacturing paraphernalia for drugs garnered a wide audience. In fact, estimates suggest that the Silk Road may have enabled over one million transactions worth an estimated $1.2 billion in revenue (Barratt, 2012). The site was dismantled in 2013 through joint law enforcement operations in the USA and Australia, though participants appeared to come from across the globe (Gibbs, 2013; Martin, 2014). A number of other markets soon emerged to take its place, including a second and third version of the original Silk Road operated by different actors (Dolliver, 2015).

Across all of the research on underground on-line economies, it is clear that the Internet is an ideal platform to successfully complete financial transactions that enable criminality. The anonymous nature of on-line spaces provides protection for the participants, yet the clear-text communications facilitate a social environment that can be used to garner trust between actors. This work is, however, growing and a range of research questions have yet to be addressed to improve our knowledge of the practices and economics of on-line markets.

This is particularly true for research on stolen data markets, as few researchers have considered their social dynamics or the economics of being a buyer or seller. Though it is clear that a range of financial service providers and individual victims are harmed around the world, there is little information on the economics of this marketplace generally. Few have provided estimates of the potential costs for data, or the economic conditions that undergird this market generally. Only two studies list prices for data and are generated from forum data (Holt & Lampke, 2010) and IRC data, respectively (Symantec, 2008). Despite the different data points, the pricing structures varied substantially with the cost for bank or credit card account details ranging from $1.30 to $500 in the forums (Holt & Lampke, 2010), to between $0.10 to $1000 depending on the information included in an IRC market (Symantec, 2008). The next most common product were credit cards with CVVs ranging from $1 to $14 in forums (Holt & Lampke, 2010), and $0.50 to $12 in IRC data (Symantec, 2008). As a result, we have minimal knowledge of the economic returns cybercriminals stand to gain from engaging in this market or its prospective impact on consumers and financial institutions generally (see Herley & Florencio, 2010).

Additionally, there is generally little research on the ways that stolen data markets are socially structured based on the interactions between buyers and sellers (Herley & Florencio, 2010; Holt, 2013; Holt & Lampke, 2010; Motoyama et al., 2011). Since people are engaging in economic transactions directly, there is the potential that stolen data markets may share similar organizational and social dynamics to that of drug markets (see Jacobs, 2000) and stolen goods markets (Stevenson, Forsythe, & Weatherburn, 2001) in the real world. For instance, some researchers have found that participants in stolen data markets seek to buy data from others with minimal long-term commitments (Dhanjani & Rios, 2008; Franklin et al., 2007; Thomas & Martin, 2006). Others have found hierarchical management structures present to regulate exchanges between participants as well as informal social control mechanisms designed to affect trust between participants (Holt & Lampke, 2010; Motoyama et al., 2011; Peretti, 2009; Wehinger, 2011).

As a result, there is a need for a systematic examination of stolen data markets to improve our knowledge of cybercrime and high-tech identity theft (Herley & Florencio, 2010; Wehinger, 2011). While most researchers approach this issue from a computer science perspective (Bacher et al., 2005; Franklin et al., 2007; Motoyama et al., 2011; Thomas & Martin, 2006; Yip et al., 2013), few have attempted to explore this issue from a criminological and sociological perspective to understand the subculture, economic, and social realities of the market and its participants. Such research is necessary to better understand the situational dynamics that shape offender practices within this market, and identify any commonalities between these virtual markets and those of illicit markets in the real world (Holt, 2013). In turn, these findings can be used to develop law enforcement strategies to disrupt existing markets, and identify policy measures that may minimize the likelihood of offender success over time (Holt, 2013; Holt & Lampke, 2010). Furthermore, the findings may speak directly to the creation of policies that can be used to better protect consumers from repeated experiences of identity theft victimization over the long term (Franklin et al., 2007; Holt & Smirnova, 2014).

The Present Study

In order to assess the economic, social, and organizational processes of stolen data markets as well as their financial impact on businesses and consumers in the global economy, this study utilizes a sample of 1990 threads generated from 13 Russian- and English-language stolen data markets where criminals and hackers buy, sell, and trade stolen financial and personal information. These forums act as on-line discussion groups where individuals can present issues or discuss problems. They are composed of threads which begin when a registered user creates a post within a forum, asking a question or making a statement (Holt, 2007, 2009; Holt & Lampke, 2010; Mann & Sutton, 1998; Motoyama et al., 2011). Other people respond to the remarks with posts of their own that are connected together to create threads. Thus, threads are composed of posts that center on a specific topic under a forum's general heading (Holt, 2007, 2009; Holt & Lampke, 2010; Motoyama et al., 2011).

The content of threads in these forums provide direct information on the quantity and range of data and services available, as well as on the payment mechanisms and communications resources used by buyers and sellers. In addition, the exchanges, evident in threads, emphasize the social nature of the market by demonstrating social ties between market actors on the basis of buying and selling activities (Herring, 2004; Holt, 2009; Holt & Lampke, 2010; Motoyama et al., 2011). Most on-line communities operate within a relational J-curve, in that a small number of forum users create the largest number of posts (Herring, 2004; Holt, 2009; Robinson, 1984). The same is true in these markets, as sellers typically made a small number of posts about their products while buyers and other market actors would make repeated posts across multiple threads. This does not discount the value of a single post, particularly when it is the only post in a thread that advertises a given product. The lack of responses demonstrates the interest of the market in such a product or service or in the bona fides of the seller. Thus, forum data demonstrates the strength of associations between participants and immediately accessible information on the practices of forum participants (Holt & Lampke, 2010; Mann & Sutton, 1998; Motoyama et al., 2011).

The sample of forums for this analysis was developed using a modified snowball sampling procedure similar to those used in traditional qualitative field work in real-world samples of interviewees (see Holt, 2007; 2010; Holt & Lampke, 2010; Wright & Decker, 1994; 1997). Data collection began with the identification of three English-language forums through Google.com using common terms in stolen data markets, including "carding dump purchase sale cvv" (Holt & Lampke, 2010; Motoyama et al., 2011). One of these sites was a sub-forum of a larger Russian-language forum. After exploring the content of threads from these sites, three Russian-language forums were identified via web links provided by forum users. Six additional forums were identified using the same processes to create a total of ten Russian-language sites and three English-language forums.

Such a tactic is valuable as there is no way to know the total universe of active stolen data markets operating around the world at any point in time (Holt, 2013; Holt & Lampke, 2010). In fact, some of these markets are well hidden from outsiders because the site operators do not allow their forum to be indexed by search engines like Google (see Holt, 2010). As a result, the only way to determine that some markets exist is by examining links to other sites provided by forum users. In turn, this can expand the representation of underground markets included in this sample.

In much the same way, five of the forums included in this sample were registration-only forums in that an individual had to create a registered user account within the site in order to access the content of the sub-forums related to data sales. Registration-restricted forums are thought to differ from that of publicly accessible forums since they add a layer of insularity from outsiders and the general public (Holt, 2010; Markham, 2011). Only those who create a username- and password-based account can see the threads within their sub-forums, unlike publicly accessible forums which display all threads to anyone who visits the site.

Since this sample includes a mix of registration-only (38.4%) and open forums (61.6%), it provides a diverse cross section of the market for stolen data. It is important to note that there are also forums operating that are completely shut off from outsiders. In fact, some forums do not allow individuals to create accounts unless they have been invited by existing members and pay a fee to gain access (Holt, 2013). As a result, the sample of forums used in this study provides a representation of more easily accessed communities but may not reflect the practices of more hidden and regulated markets operating on-line.

In order to capture the contents of the forums included in this sample, the researchers created accounts in all 13 forums but did not actually post in any of the threads. Though individuals regularly interact with one another through forums, a number of users often "lurk" or examine forum communications without actually posting. We chose to lurk in order to minimize any potential for researcher contamination (Holt, 2010; Silverman, 2013). By passively and covertly monitoring the forum threads, we reduced the potential for our identity as researchers to be revealed and otherwise affect the processes of the market (Holt, 2010; Markham, 2011). Since on-line markets are sensitive to infiltration by law enforcement and researchers (see Franklin et al., 2007; Holt & Blevins, 2007; Jenkins, 2001; Motoyama et al., 2011), this was viewed as the most fruitful avenue for data collection rather than direct engagement with buyers and sellers.

Examining the hosting locations of this sample of forums suggests they are similar to the larger composition of stolen data markets generally (see Table 1.1; Symantec, 2012). Four of the sites were hosted in Russia, and all of these sites utilized Russian as their primary language. Another was hosted in Latvia, a former member of the USSR, though its participants communicated in English and had a large proportion of ripping complaints. Europe was also a prominent host for these markets, as two were hosted in Germany, one in Luxembourg, and another in the Netherlands. One of the sites was hosted in the UK, though it utilizes the .ru country extension suggesting it is Russian. Another site was hosted in the British Virgin Islands, though the participants communicated entirely in Russian. Finally, two of the sites were hosted in the USA, though one forum's participants communicated entirely in English while the other was in Russian. It is also noteworthy that only three of the sites had their domain registered using a publicly identifiable persona including a name and email address. The rest used a private registration service to anonymize the identity of the hosting service. Thus, the mixed composition of the site hosting information relative to the participants' communication methods is reflective of the larger dynamics of the market for stolen data (Symantec, 2012).

Using these forums, the research team captured all threads posted from carding or sales-related sub-forums in order to develop a substantive

Table 1.1 Hosting detail for each forum

Forum number	Hosting country	Domain registrant	Language	Registration required
1	Germany	Private	RU	No
2	USA	Not current	ENG	No
3	USA	Private	RU	No
4	British Virgin Islands	Private	RU	No
5	UK	Private	RU	No
6	Russia	Private	RU	Yes
7	Russia	Private	RU/ENG sub	Yes
8	Latvia	Private	ENG	No
9	Russia	Public	RU/ENG sub	No
10	Germany	Public	RU	Yes
11	Russia	Private	RU	No
12	Netherlands	Private	RU	Yes
13	Luxembourg	Private	RU	Yes

volume of posts to better explore the organization of forum participants. The threads and content for each of these forums were saved as webpages, then copied, cut, and pasted into MS Word documents. A certified Russian translator with substantive experience with technological jargon and forum communications translated the Russian-language content from all forums.

Due to the availability of the translator, convenience samples of 25 threads from each Russian forum were selected to capture the most recently posted items for sale in each site (see Table 1.2). Additional samples of threads were translated from eight forums, particularly those that had active posting, in order to better assess the practices of actors and the network connectivity of participants. Due to a complication with the language encoding of threads from Forum 3, the translator was unable to completely translate all threads sampled. Thus, this forum content is excluded from both the social organization and social network analyses. Repeat threads were excluded from analysis, but translated to ensure reliability of content. The research team also oversampled threads from the English-language forums in order to capture any variations in the nature of these markets and their organizational composition. This strategy provided a mix of user populations and duration over time, while at the same time creating a relatively matched sample of posts between English- and Russian-language threads across the forums.

Table 1.2 Forum descriptive statistics

Forum	No. of threads	First post	Last post	No. of posts	No. of months
1	55	12/31/2010	7/21/2011	110	6.7
2	128	12/1/2010	2/23/2011	404	2.73
3	6	10/17/2010	7/16/2011	7	8.97
4	144	10/3/2009	12/25/2011	433	26.73
5	89	6/6/2008	12/11/2011	177	30.17
6	48	2/5/2009	11/14/2011	864	33.3
7	202	12/26/2010	7/9/2011	428	6.43
8	590	4/1/2009	11/1/2011	1239	31
9	312	4/1/2011	7/21/2011	1603	3.67
10	35	4/10/2010	3/7/2011	178	10.9
11	60	5/9/2007	2/25/2012	587	57.53
12	71	11/7/2007	11/9/2012	362	60.07
13	153	6/6/2007	7/25/2012	482	61.63

The range of time included in this sample of threads provides a wealth of information concerning the social organization of stolen data markets (see Table 1.2 for detail). To that end, six of the forums had posts over more than a two-year window, giving substantial insights into the products sold and organization of stolen data markets. Several forums contained only a few months of posts, demonstrating variations in the structure and duration of the market. As such, this sample provides a representation of the activities of buyers and sellers in stolen data markets using various languages over time.

Though this data set provides a substantive representation of the market for stolen data operating across the world over time, they are temporally bound by the practices of actors at that time. The information developed from these forums focuses primarily on the time frame between the late 2000s and 2011, limiting its utility to help us to understand the current practices of data markets. This is true of all cybercrimes, particularly hacking-related offenses such as data theft, since they evolve with the technologies available at any point in time (James, 2005; Newman & Clarke, 2003; Wall, 2007). For instance, the forms of payment accepted by sellers in stolen data markets have changed based on the availability of digital payment systems and law enforcement attempts to shutter their activities. In the mid-2000s, data thieves regularly accepted payments via an on-line payment system called e-Gold which operated out of the Caribbean and an office in Florida. This service was prosecuted under the USA PATRIOT Act as a facilitator for money transmissions without a license in 2008 (Peretti, 2009). As a result, vendors began to transition to other payment systems like Web Money and Liberty Reserve in order to accept and process payments (Holt & Smirnova, 2014).

Thus, it is vital to note that this data can only provide a snapshot of the activities of market actors during this time period. The posts analyzed may not be representative of all exchanges nor the current practices of participants in the market today. In addition, this data is not representative of more complex and hidden forums that cannot be identified via traditional search protocols. Instead, this data reflects the practices of more readily accessible markets operating to buy and sell stolen data. Finally, our findings may not be applicable to markets operating in other languages and regions of the world, such as Arabic or Asian sites. Despite these limits, the findings still provide vital information on the general activities of the market, their prospective economic impact, and the organizational practices of actors at a recent point in time.

This Work

Though the data generated from these forums is qualitative in nature, we apply both qualitative and quantitative methods to analyze the data and understand the economy, subculture, and organization of the market with quotes from the data where appropriate. Since a range of analysis techniques are employed, we discuss the distinct analysis methods used within each chapter. We also use quotes from forum posts to help illustrate various points in each chapter, though we use pseudonyms to refer to forum users to provide a modicum of anonymity for their on-line identities. Chapter 2 of this book explores the prevalence and prices of stolen personal financial information sold, as well as the process of advertising and paying for goods which shapes market interactions. Basic descriptive statistics are used to present the range of products offered, which consist primarily of various pieces of personal financial data, though services to monetize the data are also prevalent. The financial institutions and nations affected through the sale of data and financial products are also discussed to demonstrate the global scope of these markets.

Chapter 3 provides an examination of the economics of the forums, including regression models to identify the factors affecting the advertised price for stolen data. The results suggest that the social conditions of the market and the payment systems accepted by a seller affect the advertised price for data. In addition, we provide a preliminary analysis estimating the gains offenders may make from the purchase of stolen data, relative to the profits of sellers. The findings suggest that developing these estimates is fraught with potential error, though they demonstrate both buyers and sellers earn substantial profits. Data buyers may, however, earn more than sellers depending on the type of information purchased.

Chapter 4 details the social organization of these markets using a qualitative assessment of Best and Luckenbill's (1994) framework of organizational dynamics at the micro- and macro-level. This sociological model of organization identifies the actor and their encounters with others as the unit of analysis based on the presence or absence of associations with others, the existence of coordinated or purposive roles, managerial positions, and duration over time (Best & Luckenbill, 1994). Thus, this chapter considers how individual participants interact and co-offend, as well as the ways that the markets are linked and persist over time.

Chapter 5 presents a series of quantitative assessments of the organizational practices of participants within and across the forums in this sample.

Using social network analyses, this chapter considers how actors are connected based on their social ties in forum posts, and visualizes these structures. The findings demonstrate that networks vary across the forums selected, some being very loosely coupled while others have more dense connections between users. Thus, this chapter discusses the meaning of these networks for the flow of information between participants along with the ways these networks are resilient to external threats, like law enforcement.

The sixth and final chapter provides policy implications from this study for law enforcement, the financial service industry, computer security personnel, and consumers generally. The magnitude of the stolen data market affects all of these groups, demanding a diverse set of public policy initiatives designed to disrupt existing markets, deter offenders, improve existing security practices, and generally inform the common person of the threat that they face from criminals who they may otherwise never interact with in the real world. This chapter concludes with a discussion of the implications of this study for criminological researchers and theories of crime generally.

References

Barratt, M. J. (2012). Silk Road: Ebay for drugs. *Addiction, 107*, 683.

Bacher, P., Holz, T., Kotter, M., & Wicherski, G. (2005). *Tracking Botnets: Using honeynets to learn more about Bots*. The Honeynet Project and Research Alliance. Retrieved July 23, 2006 from http://www.honeynet.org/papers/bots/

Best, J., & Luckenbill, D. F. (1994). *Organizing deviance* (2nd ed.). New Jersey: Prentice Hall.

Chu, B., Holt, T. J., & Ahn, G. J. (2010). *Examining the creation, distribution, and function of malware on-line*. Technical Report for National Institute of Justice. NIJ Grant No. 2007-IJ-CX-0018. Retrieved from http://www.ncjrs.gov/pdffiles1/nij/grants/230112.pdf

Cunningham, S., & Kendall, T. (2010). Sex for sale: Online commerce in the world's oldest profession. In T. J. Holt (Ed.), *Crime online: Correlates, causes, and context* (pp. 114–140). Raleigh, NC: Carolina Academic Press.

Dhanjani, N., & Rios, B. (2008). *Bad sushi: Beating phishers at their own game*. Presented at the Annual Blackhat Meetings, Las Vegas, NV.

Dolliver, D. S. (2015). Evaluating drug trafficking on the tor network: Silk Road 2, the sequel. *International Journal of Drug Policy, 26*(11); 1113–1123.

Federal Reserve. (2013). *Consumers and Mobile Financial Services 2013*. Washington, DC: Board of Governors of the Federal Reserve. Retrieved from http://www.federalreserve.gov/econresdata/consumers-and-mobile-financial-services-report-201303.pdf

Fox, S. (2013). *51 % of U.S. Adults Bank Online*. Pew Research Center. Retrieved from http://www.pewinternet.org/2013/08/07/51-of-u-s-adults-bank-online/

Franklin, O. (2013). Unravelling the dark web. *British GQ*. Retrieved from http://www.gq-magazine.co.uk/comment/articles/2013-02/07/silk-road-online-drugs-guns-black-market/viewall

Franklin, J., Paxson, V., Perrig, A., & Savage, S. (2007). *An inquiry into the nature and cause of the wealth of internet miscreants*. Paper presented at CCS07, October 29–November 2, 2007, Alexandria, VA.

Gibbs, S. (2013). Silk Road underground market closed-but others will replace it. *The Guardian*, October 3. Retrieved from http://www.theguardian.com/technology/2013/oct/03/silk-road-underground-market-closed-bitcoin

Herley, C., & Florencio, D. (2010). Nobody sells gold for the price of silver: Dishonesty, uncertainty and the underground economy. In T. Moor, D. J. Pym, & C. Ioannidis (Eds.), *Economics of information security and privacy* (pp. 35–53). New York: Springer.

Herring, S. C. (2004). Slouching toward the ordinary: Current trends in computer-mediated communication. *New Media & Society, 6*(1), 26–36.

Higgins, K. J. (2014). Target, Neiman Marcus data breaches tip of the iceberg. *Dark Reading*, January 13. Retrieved February 17, 2014, from http://www.darkreading.com/attacks-breaches/target-neiman-marcus-data-breaches-tip-o/240165363

Holt, T. J. (2007). Subcultural evolution? Examining the influence of on- and off-line experiences on deviant subcultures. *Deviant Behavior, 28*, 171–198.

Holt, T. J. (2009). Lone hacks or group cracks: Examining the social organization of computer hackers. In F. Smalleger & M. Pittaro (Eds.), *Crimes of the Internet* (pp. 336–355). Upper Saddle River, NJ: Pearson Prentice Hall.

Holt, T. J. (2010). Exploring strategies for qualitative criminological and criminal justice inquiry using on-line data. *Journal of Criminal Justice Education, 21*, 300–321.

Holt, T. J. (2013). Exploring the social organization and structure of stolen data markets. *Global Crime, 14*, 155–174.

Holt, T. J., & Blevins, K. R. (2007). Examining sex work from the client's perspective: Assessing johns using online data. *Deviant Behavior, 28*, 333–354.

Holt, T. J., & Bossler, A. M. (2016). *Cybercrime in progress: Theory and prevention of technology-enabled offenses*. New York: Routledge Press.

Holt, T. J., & Lampke, E. (2010). Exploring stolen data markets on-line: Products and market forces. *Criminal Justice Studies, 23*, 33–50.

Holt, T. J., & Smirnova, O. (2014). *Examining the structure, organization, and processes of the international market for stolen data*. Washington, DC: US Department of Justice. Retrieved from https://www.ncjrs.gov/pdffiles1/nij/grants/245375.pdf

Holz, T., Engelberth, M., & Freiling, F. (2009). Learning more about the underground economy: A case-study of keyloggers and dropzones. In M. Backes & P. Ning (Eds.), *Computer security—ESCORICS* (pp. 1–18). Berlin and Heidelberg: Springer.

Honeynet Research Alliance. (2003). Profile: Automated credit card fraud. *Know Your Enemy Paper* series. Retrieved from http://www.honeynet.org/papers/profiles/ccfraud.pdf
Jacobs, B. (2000). *Robbing drug dealers: Violence beyond the law*. New York: Aldine de Gruyter.
James, L. (2005). *Phishing exposed*. Rockland, MA: Syngress.
Jenkins, P. (2001). *Beyond tolerance: Child pornography on the Internet*. New York: New York University Press.
Karami, M., & McCoy, D. (2013). Understanding the Emerging Threat of DDoS-as-a-Service. In Presented as part of the 6th USENIX Workshop on Large-Scale Exploits and Emergent Threats.
Krebs, B. (2011). Are megabreaches out? E-thefts downsized in 2010. *Krebs on Security, 2011.* Retrieved June 1, 2012, from http://krebsonsecurity.com/tag/heartland--payment-systems/
Li, W., & Chen, H. (2014). Identifying top sellers in the underground economy using deep learning-based sentiment analysis. *Intelligence and Security Informatics Conference*, 64–67.
Mann, D., & Sutton, M. (1998). Netcrime: More changes in the organisation of thieving. *British Journal of Criminology, 38*, 201–229.
Markham, A. N. (2011). Internet research. In D. Silverman (Ed.), *Qualitative research: Issues of theory, method, and practice* (3rd ed., pp. 111–127). Thousand Oaks, CA: Sage.
Martin, J. (2014). Lost on the Silk Road: Online drug distribution and the cryptomarket. *Criminology and Criminal Justice, 14*, 351–367.
Motoyama, M., McCoy, D., Levchenko, K., Savage, S., & Voelker, G. M. (2011). An analysis of underground forums. *IMC'11*, 71–79.
Newman, G., & Clarke, R. (2003). *Superhighway robbery: Preventing e-commerce crime*. Cullompton: Willan Press.
Peretti, K. K. (2009). Data breaches: What the underground world of "carding" reveals. *Santa Clara Computer and High Technology Law Journal, 25*, 375–413.
Provos, A. N., Mavrommatis, P., Rajab, M. A., & Monroe, F. (2008). *All your iFrames point to us*. Google Technical Report. Retrieved from http://static.googleusercontent.com/media/research.google.com/en//archive/provos-2008.pdf
Quinn, J. F., & Forsyth, C. J. (2013). Red light districts on blue screens: A typology for understanding the evolution of deviant communities on the internet. *Deviant Behavior, 34*(7), 579–585.
Roberts, P. F. (2007). Retailer TJX reports massive data breach: Credit, debit data stolen. Extent of breach still unknown. *InfoWorld*, June 4. Retrieved October 1, 2007, from http://www.infoworld.com/d/security--central/retailer-tjx--reports-massive--data-breach-953

Robinson, M. (1984). *Groups.* New York: John Wiley & Sons.
Sanders, T. (2008). Male sexual scripts intimacy, sexuality and pleasure in the purchase of commercial sex. *Sociology, 42*(3), 400–417.
Silverman, D. (2013). *Interpreting qualitative data: Methods for analyzing talk, text, and interaction* (4th ed.). Thousand Oaks, CA: Sage.
Stevenson, R. J., Forsythe, L. M. V., & Weatherburn, D. (2001). The stolen goods market in New South Wales Australia: An analysis of disposal avenues and tactics. *British Journal of Criminology, 41,* 101–118.
Symantec Corporation. (2008). *Symantec: Symantec Internet security threat report XII.* Retrieved from http://eval.symantec.com/mktginfo/enterprise/white_papers/b-whitepaper_internet_security_threat_report_xii_04-2008.en-us.pdf
Symantec Corporation. (2012). *Symantec Internet security threat report, Volume 17.* Retrieved from http://www.symantec.com/threatreport/
Target. (2014). Data breach FAQ: Answers to commonly asked questions for guests impacted by the recent data breach. Retrieved from https://corporate.target.com/about/shopping-experience/payment-card-issue-faq
Thomas, R., & Martin, J. (2006). The underground economy: Priceless. *;login: The Usenix Magazine, 31,* 7–17.
Verini, J. (2010). The great cyberheist. *The New York Times,* November 14. Retrieved from http://www.nytimes.com/2010/11/14/magazine/14Hacker-t.html?_r=1
Wall, D. S. (2007). *Cybercrime: The transformation of crime in the information age.* Cambridge: Polity Press.
Wehinger, F. (2011). The Dark Net: Self-regulation dynamics of illegal online markets for identities and related services. *Intelligence and Security Informatics Conference,* 209–213.
Wright, R. T., & Decker, S. H. (1994). *Burglars on the job: Streetlife and residential break-ins.* Boston, MA: Northeastern University Press.
Wright, R. T., & Decker, S. H. (1997). *Armed robbers in action: Stickups and street culture.* Boston, MA: Northeastern University Press.
Yip, M., Webber, C., & Shadbolt, N. (2013). Trust among cybercriminals? Carding forums, uncertainty, and implications for policing. *Policing and Society, 23,* 1–24.

CHAPTER 2

The Marketing and Sales of Stolen Data

Abstract This chapter outlines the general practices and products offered by vendors within the 13 forums sampled that constitute markets for stolen data. The most common products sold were dumps, or credit/debit card numbers, followed by CVV data, which includes credit card numbers and the three- or four-digit pin number located on the back of the card. There were a range of prices observed for these products, and differences in the nature of products sold based on the language used within the forum and the number of complaints received against disreputable vendors. The chapter concludes with a discussion of the difference in price observed by country for multiple products offered within the markets.

Keywords Dumps • CVV • Ripping • Trust • Price

Though the existing body of research suggests there are a range of products for sale in the market for stolen data, it is not clear how those products are priced, the ways that market forces may shape the cost of data, and the negotiation process generally. This chapter will provide an overview of the quantity of products offered, the sales process, and variations in the distribution of products based on the behavior of sellers. Finally, we conclude with an assessment of the countries impacted by data thieves, and any prospective variations in price by the country of origin for stolen data.

Before we discuss the market, it is necessary to detail how we classified products based on the content of the ads posted in the threads from each

© The Editor(s) (if applicable) and The Author(s) 2016
T.J. Holt et al., *Data Thieves in Action*, Palgrave Studies
in Cybercrime and Cybersecurity, DOI 10.1057/978-1-137-58904-0_2

19

forum. Specifically, a post was coded as a sale if an individual stated that they were "selling," "offering," or otherwise providing a service (see also Chu, Holt, & Ahn, 2010; Holt & Lampke, 2010; Motoyama, McCoy, Levchenko, Savage, & Voelker, 2011). Requests for data or services were coded as "buys" based on the use of language like "need a," "buying," or "seeking." In addition, products were coded separately so that we could capture the full scope of the market. If an individual sold both credit card numbers and PayPal accounts, this was treated as an individual ad for card data and PayPal accounts respectively (see also Holt & Lampke, 2010). In addition to the advertisements or requests that started a thread, we also coded any additional ad or update that appeared within the thread to capture variations in content over time as well as any potential competitors who posted within a sales thread.

Our coding strategy created a total number of advertisements ($N=12,844$) that was larger than the overall number of threads where they appeared. The overwhelming majority of ads were focused on sales (95.7%), suggesting that the market is saturated with products and there is minimal need for overt solicitations for information (Franklin, Paxson, Perrig, & Savage, 2007; Holt & Lampke, 2010; Motoyama et al., 2011). The usernames, email addresses, forms of payment accepted, and the sellers' terms of service were also captured to better document the practices of forum actors.

This chapter will present descriptive statistics regarding the advertised prices for each code, as well as any additional information concerning the country of origin for data and the financial institution harmed. Information will also be presented concerning the preferred payment systems used by buyers and sellers, as well as contact methods to communicate outside of the forums. The advertised price for data will also be detailed in US dollars as this was the most common currency used. Any price listed in rubles was converted using the estimated value of the currency in US dollars on that day. The logistic regression models will be presented to assess the impact of social and market forces on the advertised price for data. Finally, the data will also be represented by countries.

The Distribution of Products in the Market

The products and services listed in each thread were coded into categories based on common aspects of the item or service offered, using common terms evident in the research literature on stolen data markets when possible (see Table 2.1 for detail; Franklin et al., 2007; Holt & Lampke, 2010; Holz, Engelberth, & Freiling, 2009; Honeynet Research Alliance,

Table 2.1 Distribution of products based on buying and selling posts

Product	Total	% of all ads	Buying posts	% of total	Selling posts	% of total
Bank accounts	205	1.60	21	10.20	184	89.80
Cash-out services	235	1.80	74	31.50	161	68.50
CVV	4481	34.90	21	0.50	4460	99.50
Dedicated servers	157	1.20	0	0	157	100.00
Drops for laundering	165	1.30	59	35.80	106	64.20
Dumps	5737	44.70	68	1.20	5669	98.80
eBay/PayPal	183	1.40	17	9.30	166	90.70
Equipment	198	1.50	12	6.10	186	93.90
Fullz	122	0.90	3	2.50	119	97.50
Identity documents	89	0.70	37	41.60	52	58.40
Malware	183	1.40	31	16.90	152	83.10
Money transfers	303	2.40	20	6.60	283	93.40
Other financial products	10	0.10	0	0.00	10	100.00
Other products	277	2.20	113	40.80	164	59.20
Personal info and accounts	99	0.80	39	39.40	60	60.60
Plastics	153	1.20	13	8.50	140	91.50
Skimmers	125	1.00	10	8.00	115	92.00
Spam and scams	122	0.90	15	12.30	107	87.70

2003; Motoyama et al., 2011). The majority of ads involved some type of stolen data (84.3%), particularly dumps and CVVs, which includes credit card information plus the three- or four-digit CVV physically located on the back of the card. This piece of information is necessary when making a purchase on-line or over the telephone so as to guarantee that the individual has the card in hand at the time of the transaction. This was exemplified in the following advertisement from Forum 8:

> **Vendmaster: Selling CCV: German/ Italy/ USA/ UK/ Netherlands/**
> Greetings,
> Selling CCV: Germany, Italy, USA, UK, Netherlands
> German cc [credit card]: 15USD
> Italy CC: 15USD
> USA CC: 6USD
> UK Without DOB [Cardholder's Date Of Birth]: 14USD
> UK with DOB: 30USD
> Netherlands: 15USD

Note: We sell all unused/Untouch cc to our Customers! to ensure Quality we sell each cc to each person! And we fully Replace cc in 48 Hours of Delivery TIME
We Accept CC orders only by WU at the moment!
Min order: 350usd
for Orders please e-mail me or add me in your messenger either you can pm me.

Sellers also offered information such as eBay and PayPal account details, as well as bank account login information, such as username, password, and secret question responses. Such data is restrictive for a prospective buyer as they have to know how to effectively utilize the data to either make purchases or engage in transfers, though it can still provide means to engage in fraud and theft.

The next most common product set involved resources that could manipulate stolen data to obtain funds from accounts or financial services (7.4%) (Franklin et al., 2007; Herley & Florencio, 2010; Holt & Lampke, 2010; Wehinger, 2011). Manipulation services can be also operated in the real world and on-line. In the real world, individuals could take cards imprinted with stolen credit or debit card data and use those cards at stores and ATMs to get currency. This is a somewhat risky process as any activity off-line exposes actors to law enforcement and prospective detection. As a result, there were a robust number of service providers who operated services to obtain funds or products through the use of stolen data. For instance, a service provider in Forum 1 offered encashment services, where he would perform transfers between financial institutions using stolen data in order to obtain cash for his clients. He explained his services through the following post:

> We are the experience team [name removed] working in the area of banking innovations, and here on the site we are ready to offer you the following services:
> We in cash funds in the RF [Russian Federation] which we have received as electronic bank transfers.
> Help with encashment: direct scheme- no intermediaries
> -encashment of funds
> -Transmit of electronic funds
> -Diversion of funds
> -Work with accounts that have been seized by the authorities
> -Work with dirty funds [acquired through illegal means of any sort]…

A number of service providers also offered a hybrid of real and virtual world processes called drops. In this instance, a drops provider would facilitate the purchase of goods using stolen data and have them shipped to real-world locations that are separate from the actual billing address of the cardholder. Once received, the items are either kept by the user or pawned, fenced, resold to obtain cash. This is a somewhat complex process, and so drops coordinators would provide specific details about their processes, as in this post from DROPS4U:

> **Drops in Europe and USA 35%**
> We are pleased to offer customers high-quality drop service in the U.S. and Europe, which ceased to be private for a narrow circle of individuals becomes public.
> Drop in the U.S.:
> About the service:
> Drop shall send to any name with shops and aukov.
> All drops pass a preliminary check.
> Personal drop most active.
> User-friendly admin facility to track the movement of goods and the state of [money] mules [who carry and launder funds].
> Permanent office support.
> Payment:
> Payment WMZ 30-35% of mine. PG/Bizrate within 72 hours Delivered. The payment comes on the status of the USPS International Dispatch, usually 24 hours after sending the mules.
> 50/50 Working on the system - almost all categories of goods. Your part will be sent to the address at our expense. Customs do not.
> accepted:
> 35% - Notebook, Sony, Apple. SLR / Lenses Canon, Nikon. Another technique Apple - iMac, MacMini, iPhone, iPad, Apple displays.
> 30% - Notebook, HP, Toshiba, Asus, Acer. Canon, Nikon. On the rest of the pre-negotiated percentage of the goods in ICQ.
> The main conditions:
> We only accept new merchandise BRAND NEW.
> The minimum cost of sending $ 300.
> If within 4 working days from the date of issuance, on the drop was not sent the goods, the drop is transferred to another person.
> Clarify the status of loot, if you have not kept sending him with a break of more than 5 working days and make sure of its condition in the admin center.
> Sending no tracks, and driven into the admin center after Delivered, only in case of confirmation of receipt of mules.

In the case of mules possible compensation of up to 15% of the mines. PG/Bizrate within a week. We do not pay compensation in case of arrival/ Call the police, FBI, and other services as well as in the case of a call from the shop goes online/Seller with auctions. In each of these cases provides comprehensive information about the drop, including the full correspondence.

The preponderance of data manipulation services may stem from the fact that data buyers may have insufficient knowledge of how to effectively use the information they have the potential to purchase. As a result, entrepreneurial hackers have filled an important niche within this market to facilitate cybercrimes for those who may not be willing to use the data they have, or are not aware of how to do so in an efficient fashion.

Finally, a number of products were advertised that individuals could use to either acquire or manipulate personal data. This includes spam distribution services, web hosting services for shops and websites, and ancillary materials and resources that could be used to engage in fraud and cybercrime generally. For instance, the following advertisement details an individual service provider who would send out spam using data that you register in order to engage in dating scams to attract lonely victims and defraud them:

> I offered your attention services for filling up your mailboxes with pindosy [people from NATO countries, esp. USA].
> the price of one response to the mailbox is 0.6 wmz
> countries ONLY UK USA CA DE FR IT. I register a profile with your data on for-pay sites... using programs such as "Tasker" and many others, I spam all the pindosy who are online on the sites with a request to write me by e-mail , a four line teaser ... Within 1 hour my program spans around 8k profiles.
> An e-mail database from for-pay sites is also available:
> USA - 14k
> DE - 8k
> uk - 21k
> fr - 3k
> it - 43k
> database validity from 6%-20% . Price for 1k-15 wmz
> I sell strictly to one person.
> If you have questions then please contact me by icq 982–374 on the net 12 hours a day.

This sort of email-based scam is quite common, and can cause victims a good deal of economic harm (Whitty, 2013; Whitty & Buchanan, 2012). As a result, these forums clearly provide individuals with all the resources necessary to engage in cybercrime and data theft from start to finish at relatively low prices (Herley & Florencio, 2010; Wehinger, 2011).

THE ADVERTISING PROCESS AND DISTRIBUTION OF PRODUCTS ON THE MARKET

The threads created across all of these forums were designed to serve as an advertisement for a seller's products or services (see also Franklin et al., 2007; Holt & Lampke, 2010; Motoyama et al., 2011). The Thread Starter, or TS, would provide a detailed description of their goods or services, products' details, pricing structures, any rules regarding the sale, and their contact and payment information. This is best demonstrated in a post from Forum 4, where an individual sold dumps or bank and credit card account information from around the world. This seller provides a range of dumps by the type of account with variable prices. Specifically, Visa and MasterCard classic cards from the USA which have a lower general balance are sold at a lower price than gold and platinum accounts, and business/corporate cards:

    Dumps Fresh Base ... EU-USA-CANADA-ASIA-OTHER. Best Valid.
    Virgin dumps: Europe, Asia, Canada, Usa and other country! We offer very good quality. Thanks All.
    PRICE LIST:
    *************USA***************
    1pcs CLASSIC/STANDARD = 20$
    1pcs GOLD/PLATINUM = 25$
    1pcs BUSINESS/SIGNATURE/PURCHASE/CORPORATE/WORLD = 30$
    1pcs AMEX = 20$
    ************CANADA************
    1pcs CLASSIC/STANDARD = 50$
    1pcs GOLD/PLATINUM/BUSINESS/SIGNATURE/PURCHASE/CORPORATE/WORLD = 70-200$
    *******EUROPE & ASIA & LATIN & OTHERS*********
    ---[code 101 - non chip]--- [This indicates the dump contains only magnetic strip data, not the chip/pin data common in cards from other nations]

1pcs CLASSIC/STANDART = 110$
1pcs GOLD/PLATINUM = 130$
1pcs BUSINESS/SIGNATURE/PURCHASE/CORPORATE/WORLD = 150$
1pcs INFINITE = 200$
****
----[code 201 - chip]---- [This indicates the dump contains the chip/pin data common in cards from other nations]
1pcs CLASSIC/STANDART = 50$
1pcs GOLD/PLATINUM = 65$
1pcs BUSINESS/SIGNATURE/PURCHASE/CORPORATE/WORLD = 120$
1pcs INFINITE = 150$
RULES:
(please read the rules carefully and follow all the steps, anyone breaking this rules shall expect to be fully ignored by service)
1. Contact with one of the our supports and choose dumps u want.
2. Calculate total price and submit your order.
3. Send us money and your e-mail.
4. We have 24 hours (maximum) to complete your order. (LR [Liberty Reserve Payment] INSTANT DELIEVERY)
5. We replace only Pickup/Hold Call Dumps with in 24 hours after time period we are not responsible
PAYMENT INFO:
LIBERTY RESERVE
Support Icq: [removed]

This post demonstrates the wide range of information and countries available for purchase by actors within the market. In fact, dumps comprised the most common item sold within this sample of forums, though there was substantial variation in the pricing for dump data (see Table 2.2 for detail). The average advertised price for dumps was much higher ($102.60) than that of the second most prevalent item, CVVs ($26.21) (see also Franklin et al., 2007; Holt & Lampke, 2010). The average price for CVV data was advertised at a slightly lower price than eBay and PayPal accounts ($27.25).

As a whole, the prices for data were lower than those of data manipulation services such as identity documents ($138.46), drops ($192.37), cash-out services ($1076.93), and money transfers ($1424.59). Skimmers, used to capture data in the field, had the highest average price at $2382.60 (see also Holt & Lampke, 2010). Products related to data capture, such as spam ($96.33), dedicated servers ($100.97), and malware ($183.27),

Table 2.2 Pricing information for products sold

Product	Min price	Max price	Mean price	SD price	Count with price	%	Count with no price	%	Percent rather than price	%
Bank accounts	5.00	700.00	198.44	153.69	63	30.7	142	69.3	2	1.0
Cash-out services	0.30	6000.00	1076.93	1963.05	14	6.0	221	94.0	63	26.8
CVV	1.00	8000.00	26.22	207.02	4316	96.3	165	3.7	0	0
Dedicated servers	0.20	700.00	100.97	196.19	42	26.7	115	73.3	0	0
Drops for laundering	0.50	1000.00	192.37	250.54	27	16.4	138	83.6	62	37.6
Dumps	0.04	8000.00	102.61	466.53	5167	90.1	570	9.9	4	0.1
eBay/PayPal	0.20	800.00	27.25	80.86	118	64.4	65	35.6	3	1.6
Equipment	3.00	5000.00	549.51	1042.86	61	30.8	137	69.2	0	0
Fullz	15.00	150.00	72.82	50.13	87	71.3	35	28.7	0	0
Identity documents	0.50	500.00	138.46	127.70	32	40.0	57	60.0	0	0
Malware	2.00	1570.00	99.60	183.27	99	54.1	84	45.9	0	0
Money transfers	10.00	38,000.00	1424.59	6188.34	37	12.2	266	87.8	85	28.1
Other financial products	6.00	15.00	10.75	3.77	4	40.0	6	60.0	0	0
Other products	0.11	5000.00	177.27	610.26	82	33.2	195	66.8	6	2.2
Personal info and accounts	1.00	5025.00	197.19	761.73	44	44.4	55	55.6	3	3.0
Plastics	0.50	3000.00	261.47	603.73	47	30.7	106	69.3	0	0
Skimmers	200.00	9000.00	2382.61	2340.68	23	18.4	102	81.6	0	0
Spam and scams	8.00	600.00	96.33	133.91	24	16.4	98	83.6	4	3.3

were also more expensive than financial data; this is in line with existing research (Dhanjani & Rios, 2008; Chu et al., 2010; Holz et al., 2009).

The price differentials may stem from two factors. First, data acquired through breaches or phishing incidents are extremely time sensitive because the account information may be closed by the originating financial institution. Vendors who can clearly and quickly communicate the range of data they have and from what countries may be more easily able to attract customers and turn a profit. Data manipulation services are dependent mostly on the ability to access an account and do not face the same temporal limitations, making their prices more negotiable dependent on the needs of the seller or buyer.

A second and salient point is that the majority of vendors for products other than data sales did not include pricing details in their advertisements (see also Chu et al., 2010; Holt & Lampke, 2010). Instead, they described the prices for services as a percentage of the total amount of money they may be asked to convert or move between accounts (see Holt & Lampke, 2010). Such a measure is practical as giving a specific price point may shortchange either the vendor by charging too little to move a large amount of money or the client by overcharging on small figures. Instead, prorating prices on the basis of the total value gives both parties a point of negotiation and parity.

Connecting Buyers and Sellers

Though the forums and threads serve as an advertising space, the actual sale of data and services takes place outside of the forums (Franklin et al., 2007; Herley & Florencio, 2010; Holt & Lampke, 2010; Motoyama et al., 2011). The hidden nature of the negotiation process makes it difficult to determine the actual prices individuals pay for information or services, and is a complicating factor in estimating the economics of these markets (Herley & Florencio, 2010; Holt & Lampke, 2010; Holt, Smirnova, & Chua, 2013). One of the most common and preferred methods of contact listed in all advertisements was ICQ ($N=8000$; 58.2%, see Table 2.3), a sort of IM protocol that is extremely popular among the Russian hacker community and within data markets specifically (Chu et al., 2010; Holt & Lampke, 2010; Holt, Strumsky, Smirnova, & Kilger, 2012). ICQ is currently owned by a Russian service provider, which may increase its attractiveness to users in this region because their records may not be readily accessed by US law enforcement.

Table 2.3 Personal contact details indicated by posters

Contact method	N	%
Email	9121	71.00
AOL	16	0.10
Gmail	250	1.80
Hotmail	645	4.70
Other	1123	8.20
Rambler	21	0.20
Yahoo	7055	51.40
Yandex	11	0.10
ICQ	8000	62.20
Jabber	231	1.70
Email and ICQ	3911	30.40
ICQ and Jabber	183	1.40

Note: Figures do not add to 100% as sellers could indicate the use of one or multiple service providers for contacts. Thus, there is substantive missing data.

The majority of individuals indicated their willingness to use email ($N=9121$; 71%), though there was some variation in the types of email providers preferred. The most common account types used by vendors were Yahoo email addresses, though a number (8.2%) used more esoteric and uncommon email providers. A small proportion ($N=231$; 1.7%) of posters also indicated that they used Jabber, an IM protocol, to communicate with buyers. The use of email and other IM clients may be less valued by buyers and sellers because they may be more difficult to anonymize and encrypt relative to a program like ICQ (Chu et al., 2010; Holt & Lampke, 2010). A number of sellers also maximized their potential for contact by utilizing ICQ and at least one form of email ($N=3911$; 30.4%), though a small proportion advertised both an ICQ and Jabber account ($N=183$; 1.4%).

In addition to contact details, approximately 25.8% of sellers advertised their preferred payment systems within a thread. Though a majority of ads did not indicate any specific payment preference, this may be due to the fact that sellers commonly accepted a proportion of a payment in the case of data acquisition services. Of those who indicated a preferred payment format, the majority accepted and used electronic payment systems (28.3%) that allow for direct transfers of funds between two parties (see also Franklin et al., 2007; Herley & Florencio, 2010; Holt & Lampke, 2010; Wehinger, 2011). The most common payment systems within this sample were Liberty Reserve ($N=2304$; 16.8%) and Web Money ($N=1528$; 11.1%). A very small proportion also accepted payments via Yandex ($N=64$; 0.4%) owned and operated by the Russian Internet search engine and service provider of the same name.

Approximately 25% of sellers accepted payments through Western Union ($N=2673$; 19.5%) or MoneyGram ($N=864$; 6.3%), which requires the sender to physically provide money, a name, the name of the recipient, and their location. In turn, this information is sent to a specified location, and the recipient must show either identification or a pre-arranged password (negotiated by the sender and the company) to receive the cash funds. The use of a physical wire transfer service adds a layer of complexity to the payment process as an intermediary may be used to travel to a physical location to send and receive funds (Chu et al., 2010; Holt & Lampke, 2010). Alternatively, the individuals sending and receiving payments may use fake identity documents in order to facilitate the transfers without using their actual identification.

The general preference among data sellers and service providers for electronic payments may be due to the fact that any transaction can be easily anonymized or sent through fraudulently created accounts to shield the identity of all participants. In fact, 1067 ads indicated that the seller would accept at least two forms of electronic payments, and 2332 (17%) of all sellers indicated that they would accept both on- and off-line payment methods.

Finally, a small proportion of ads ($N=373$; 2.7%) noted that they would accept guarantors or escrow payment systems. Though this is a small proportion, these ads were present across 11 of the 13 forums suggesting it is an accepted process. Guarantor and escrow systems may provide additional layer of trust, as this sort of payment requires an intermediary to hold money on behalf of the buyer until such time as the seller releases the requested merchandise (Herley & Florencio, 2010; Holt & Lampke, 2010; Wehinger, 2011). Once the buyer confirms they have received their purchase, the guarantor releases the funds to the seller. This quote from Forum 7 details the process of guarantor and escrow agents:

Escrow service
Escrow only insures money at time (fixed time) transactions.
All terms of deal negotiated between the parties. Escrow they spend is not necessary.
Escrow doesn't check goods or services.
The principle of insurance transactions:

1. Buyer pays Indemnitor amount of transaction and fees for escrow service. Reports icq number for which this sum is intended.
P.S. Under arrangement escrow fee may pay any member of transaction.
2. Escrow confirms receipt of money to another party.
3. The seller (service) provides direct product (or service) to another party to transaction without participation of Escrow.
4. After receipt and verification of goods (providing services) buyer contacts the Escrow and to announce completion of transaction.
5. Escrow pays money to seller (service).
Escrow service fee:
>500$ - 8%
<500$ - 6%
3000$ and more - 5%

Escrow or guarantor payments provide a valuable but optional mechanism to reduce the risk of being cheated by unscrupulous sellers. Specifically, buyers have no guarantee that they will receive products after sending payment. There are minimal resources available for buyers in the event that they are cheated by a seller, thus the use of guarantors increases the likelihood of a successful transaction and promotes trust between buyers and sellers (Herley & Florencio, 2010; Holt & Lampke, 2010; Wehinger, 2011).

Since data sales and services require some degree of technical skill to be successfully used, a number of sellers promoted the resources they would make available to buyers as a measure of customer service and support in their ads (see also Holt & Lampke, 2010; Wehinger, 2011). There was some variation in the practices of sellers based on the product or service they offered. For instance, this seller offered PayPal, eBay, or bank account login credentials and indicated how they would assist customers in using data purchased:

> We are the trusted sellers of the PayPal accounts… Here are some of the rules of the service:
> Seller is not responsible for sm (security measures); we check all the accounts manually prior [to] giving them to you. You'll also get a clean socks5 [proxy connection to access the account on-line]
> Seller is not responsible for the unsuccessfull [SIC] usage of the account.
> We may exchange your account in case the password won't match. Please inform us promptly!
> Please provide us with the screenshot in all the weird situations…
> You're free to do whatever you want to do with the account that you've bought. We take no responsibility on your further actions.

Though this vendor stipulated that customers were responsible for the use of data purchased, they would also give free proxies and offer exchanges of bad information in the event it was due to an error on their part. Product replacements were a somewhat common technique among vendors ($N=4285$; 31.2%) in order to ensure customers were satisfied with their purchases (Franklin et al., 2007; Herley & Florencio, 2010; Holt & Lampke, 2010; Wehinger, 2011). This is most likely a result of the fact that credit and debit card information may be deactivated by the cardholder or the issuing financial institution before it could be used by a thief. To that end, sellers would indicate a specific window of time during which a customer could obtain replacements. One seller in Forum 2 indicated he would "exchange invalids within 1 hour," though the majority of sellers allowed 24 hours for replacements.

A small proportion of vendors ($N=305$; 2.2%) would also provide prospective customers with a free sample of data or a test of their products (see Franklin et al., 2007; Herley & Florencio, 2010; Holt & Lampke, 2010). For instance, a dumps vendor may post an example of the structure of their data, which would typically include the card type, account number, three digit security code, expiration data, as well as cardholder name and address (Herley & Florencio, 2010). Posting a sample in this fashion may be attractive for some buyers as it could demonstrate the structure of their information or validate claims of the quality of their data (Franklin et al., 2007; Thomas & Martin, 2006). Some researchers have, however, argued that publicly posting information is actually a tactic employed by unreliable sellers to attract unskilled buyers (Herley & Florencio, 2010). By giving away data, a seller loses money and reduces their productivity by responding to requests for free information (Herley & Florencio, 2010; Wehinger, 2011). As a result, reputable vendors may not offer free tests of data in order to retain as much of their profit margin as is possible.

A number of sellers ($N=883$; 6.4%) noted in their ads that they operated specialized customers service lines via ICQ or email, or would assist buyers after a purchase (Holt & Lampke, 2010; Wehinger, 2011). The use of customer service lines reinforces the notion that some buyers may have limited knowledge of how to use data that they can purchase within the market. Such a measure may prove valuable to retain customers over time, particularly those who are unable to use data to the best of their ability. Customer service mechanisms may also be important for money laundering services so that buyers can readily obtain status updates on transactions from the service provider.

A very small proportion of sellers ($N=357$; 2.6%) also went through the process of having products tested and reviewed by forum moderators. A number of forums offered vendors the option to have their products tested, where the seller gives a sample of data or a service to forum moderators who assess the validity of the sellers' claims (Holt & Lampke, 2010; Wehinger, 2011). Once the test is complete, the moderator posts their review in the seller's thread to demonstrate that the individual is reliable. In turn, prospective customers can know that they will not be cheated by an unreliable seller (discussed further in Chap. 4). The rarity of product testing may stem from the fact that most markets are unregulated and are unable to support the complexity needed for product testing (Herley & Florencio, 2010; Wehinger, 2011).

Since sales took place outside of the forums, buyers had to find ways to determine what vendors were trustworthy and reliable. Advertisements regarding the customer service options supported by a vendor were helpful but provided no guarantee that their data was reliable. Thus, buyers in these forums were encouraged to provide feedback about their interactions with a seller in that particular thread (Holt & Lampke, 2010; Motoyama et al., 2011). Information about exchanges is invaluable as the comments provide one of the only real mechanisms for dispute management and resolution.

Should an individual complete a transaction, the forum moderators and vendors wanted their customers to provide a post about their experience so that others could use this information to determine who is trustworthy. Positive comments were noted in almost 12% of ads ($N=1575$; 11.5%) and helped to demonstrate the quality of a seller's product. This can be illustrated with the following feedback posted for a dumps seller:

Famo: Awesome!!!!!!!!!!!!! His dumps work with high amounts, 5/5 valid A++++++++
LEGIT SELLER!!!
Benefit: Very Good Person...
Top Dump Seller A+++
Famo: Again and again i trust this guy, bought 50pcs UAE [United Arab Emirates], he gived [SIC] me +5 in bonuse[s], 49 [cards] was valid, 6 [inactive accounts] replaced without questions! He is awesome, his dumps work on very high amounts! Good luck in ur bis [business] bro! TNX U BRO!

Such information is extremely valuable for other buyers to know who to seek services from. A larger proportion of negative comments were identified in ads ($N=2467$; 18%), suggesting that a vendor was not reliable. This was exemplified in a series of posts from Forum 4, where a seller named Jackson sold credit card data from various countries and received substantial negative feedback because of his use of bad data and poor response times. Prospective and actual customers noted this in their posts, stating:

> **Stan**: They have been selling the same dump since April, very stale, support is no help!
> **Nickly**: yes Stan bulshit [SIC] garbage dumps in his shop…all claims dumps there are dead since April and is still claiming 90 percent valid… lol buyer be careful
> **Vendor**: dumps extremely low working % You will be lucky to card yourself a happy meal with one of these shit ass dumps… Thumbs down.

In the event that a buyer was truly dissatisfied by their interaction with a seller, one of the most important phrases they could use in their feedback was the term "ripper," "donkey," or "scammer" (Franklin et al., 2007; Herley & Florencio, 2010; Holt & Lampke, 2010; Honeynet Research Alliance, 2003; Motoyama et al., 2011). These terms signify that either (1) a seller did not provide anything in return for payment or (2) their service or data was of extremely poor quality. For instance, an individual in Forum 8 created a thread saying:

> I have been ripped off three times, so bad and I don't have any money left right now. what should I do? one of scammer named [removed] i was trust him, i bought 3 cvv from EU for test him, he did give to me, the second time, I ordered wu transfer. he never give to me, just took my money away.

In this case, the buyer was completely cheated as they got nothing from the seller despite providing him with a payment. As a result, the buyer has no way to get those funds back or any legal recourse against the buyer for misrepresentation (Herley & Florencio, 2010).

The appearance of the term "ripper" or "ripped off" demonstrates to prospective buyers that a vendor is unreliable, and should not be used due to an increased risk of loss or negative experiences (Franklin et al., 2007; Herley & Florencio, 2010; Holt & Lampke, 2010; Wehinger, 2011). Since there are so many vendors for the same products across all of these forums, it is plausible that a trustworthy seller may not yet have feedback for their products. This leaves buyers with the difficult task of determining if a seller is trustworthy based mostly on the content of an advertisement within a thread. There are, however, no immediate cues within the language of an ad that an individual may be a ripper. This issue was exemplified in a post from Forum 8 where an individual tried to explain how rippers might structure their posts to attract buyers:

> -ripper wants to receive the money as fast as possible and he doesn't care of the final [outcome] of deal; so the first main sign of ripper – desiring to receive the money fast, he thinks out a lot of reasons for this – pregnant wife, blocked keeper, drop's worrying etc
> -ripper wants to be shown as well-knowing guy so he uses a lot of terms and specific words;
> -nickname; often greed and fieriness [fireiness] can be read in ripper's nick which are changing like a gloves, so asa [SIC] we see Ecspress, Fast, Easy etc and almos[t] with the words "money", "cash" etc we should be careful already and begin to verify this person.
> -Number of posts – potential ripper usually has too little posts for his registration date or too much posts – tries to make it's number more. It's also recommended to read what the person posts about on forums and make conclusion about his mind, if there are stupid posts or posts without any meanings – make conclusion yourself.
> -A lot of rippers usually post at the and [end] of there [SIC] posts "escrow accepted". But when you talk that you want to work through escrow he usually finds lots of reasons don't work through it.
> Conclusion: none of these things can tell you that this guy is ripper. But in combination it gets you the information about him and it's better don't deal with such guy.

This quote demonstrates that there is no single way to identify a ripper based on their advertisement, and it also underscores the overall community concern over the rippers. Buyers must carefully review and cultivate information about a vendor before engaging in a transaction, and even then they may be ripped off (Franklin et al., 2007; Holt & Lampke, 2010; Motoyama et al., 2011; Wehinger, 2011). As a result, reviews of sellers are one of the only real ways that buyers can identify who is reputable. And even then rippers can post positive feedback for themselves using fictitious user profiles further distorting the information.

Seven forums in this sample (53.8%) had users post feedback using terms related to ripping, suggesting it is a common problem within the market. However, only one seller received complaints of ripping in four of the seven forums. Such a small number of complaints may be reasonable given that it is difficult to ensure all sellers in any market are reputable (Herley & Florencio, 2010; Holt & Lampke, 2010; Wehinger, 2011). A much larger proportion of sellers were purported to be rippers in the remaining two forums. For example, Forum 4 had approximately 16% of threads with ripper complaints, while complaints were noted in more than 30% of all threads in Forums 2 and 8.

Due to the large percentage of complaints evident in these two forums, they will be considered ripping forums in the remainder of this book. This classification is necessary due to the need to understand any different dynamics evident in ripping and non-ripping forums. In fact, the economists Herley and Florencio (2010) argue that ripping forums are more likely to have lower pricing for products which lead to ultimately higher costs for buyers because of the difficulty in obtaining usable products. This is evident in our data when we separate the products sold by ripping and non-ripping forums, as there are pertinent differences in the products sold (see Table 2.4). While dumps are the most common product sold between both ripping and non-ripping forums, CVVs were more overwhelmingly sold in forums with ripping complaints (see Herley & Florencio, 2010). As a result, ripping forums may be driven by fictitious ads for products that are viewed as attractive to inexperienced buyers.

To further explore any differences in the nature of the forums, products were separated based on the use of either English or Russian languages by participants (see Table 2.5). Dumps and CVVs were the most common products sold in all forums, though they were most commonly sold in

Table 2.4 Top ten products sold by forum type

Including all forums			Excluding two forums		
Product type	N	%	Product type	N	%
Dumps	5735	44.7	Dumps	2748	63.6
CVV	4481	34.9	Cash-out services	196	4.5
Money Xfer	303	2.4	Other products	170	3.9
Other products	277	2.2	Malware	151	3.5
Cash-out services	235	1.8	Dedicated hosting	139	3.2
Bank accounts	205	1.6	Drops	136	3.1
Equipment	198	1.5	Money transfers	127	2.9
Malware/eBay, PayPal	183	1.4	eBay and PayPal	108	2.5
Drops	165	1.3	Spam/scam materials	104	2.4
Dedicated hosting	157	1.2	Plastics	86	2.0

Table 2.5 Product distribution by forum language

Product	English	%	Russian	%	Total
Bank accounts	171	83.4	34	16.6	205
Cash-out service	102	43.4	133	56.6	235
CVV	4456	99.4	25	0.6	4481
Dedicated hosting	29	18.5	128	81.5	157
Drops	96	58.1	69	41.9	165
Dumps	5381	93.8	356	6.2	5737
eBay/PayPal accounts	94	51.4	89	48.6	183
Equipment	126	63.6	72	36.4	198
Fullz	121	99.2	1	0.8	122
Identity documents	68	76.4	21	23.6	89
Malware	33	18.00	150	82.00	183
Money transfer	264	87.1	39	12.9	303
Other financial product	10	100.0	0	0.0	10
Other product	126	45.5	151	54.5	277
Personal accounts	40	40.4	59	59.6	99
Plastics	112	73.2	41	26.8	153
Skimmer	125	100.0	0	0.0	125
Spam/scam materials	26	21.3	96	78.7	122
Total	11,380	88.4	1464	11.6	12,844

English-language forums. This may also reflect the problem of ripping, as the forums with the greatest number of complaints regarding rip-offs primarily communicated in English. Buyers who are inexperienced or unfamiliar with the process of acquiring and using stolen data may first identify forums through the use of Google searches and similar keywords as those used in this study. They may not know how to identify more legitimate or hidden markets with a greater degree of legitimate vendors, thereby increasing their willingness to make purchases from ripping forums. When the buyers see the sellers' low advertised prices for dumps or account data, they may be inclined to make a purchase (see Herley & Florencio, 2010).

Other products were more evenly distributed across the two languages, including eBay and PayPal accounts, personal accounts, other products, and cash-out services. These products may not be as attractive for rippers, especially cash-out services, as the provider may not be able to acquire an immediate payment as would otherwise be possible with dumps or CVV data. Russian-language forums had a much larger proportion of products related to the acquisition of data, including hosting services, malware, and spam and scam materials. As a result, the distribution of products suggests that there may be multiple markets operating that are separated by the language of the participants (Herley & Florencio, 2010; Wehinger, 2011). A final issue was noted in classifying ripping and non-ripping forums. While each thread was treated as an individualized advertising space for the seller who created it, some users would advertise their products in another seller's thread. This practice, called hijacking, was viewed as unacceptable because the hijacker might draw customers away from the TS. Hijacking was viewed as generally unacceptable in legitimate forums because it disadvantages the TS and creates competition, and was banned in three of the forums (Wehinger, 2011). Though hijacking was generally limited in this sample of threads (10.4%), there was a significant difference in the number of hijacking found in the ripping and non-ripping forums (Chi-square = 31.104; sig = 0.000). In fact, 7.2% of hijacking incidents were observed in ripping forums relative to only 3.2% in non-ripping forums. As a result, hijacking incidents appear to be related to the legitimacy of a forum and its advertisers, and supports the presence of market segmentation (Herley & Florencio, 2010; Holt, 2013).

Exploring the Origins of Stolen Data

Given the tremendous number of ads related to data sales, there is a need to understand what nations were most affected by data thieves. The overwhelming majority of data sold appeared to originate from Canada, European nations, and the USA respectively (see Table 2.6 for detail). All of these regions have a large proportion of their population using debit and credit cards to make purchases on a daily basis (Verision, 2012). As a result, the number of potential targets for compromise is disproportionately greater in these nations. Furthermore, these areas are commonly affected by data breaches that increase the risk of data exposure (Holt & Lampke, 2010; Symantec, 2012; Verision, 2012).

Some previous studies of stolen data markets have found the majority of data sold originated from US consumers (Franklin et al., 2007; Holt & Lampke, 2010), though that is not the case in this data set. While US data is present, it is somewhat less than that of European nations depending on the nature of the data sold. In fact, some argue that US data should be more plentiful because US citizens tend to hold multiple credit cards with higher balances than those in Europe (Newman & Clarke, 2003). In addition, there are fewer restrictions and government mandates on the secure storage and transmission of electronic payment information in the USA

Table 2.6 Location of stolen data by product

Location of data	Bank accounts	%	CVV	%	Dumps	%	Fullz	%
Asia	11	9.2	174	4.0	473	8.7	10	9.2
Australia/New Zealand	4	3.3	284	6.3	152	2.8	8	7.3
Canada	23	19.3	411	9.2	675	12.5	13	11.9
Europe	48	40.3	1278	29.0	1598	29.6	45	41.3
Other	7	5.9	154	3.4	664	12.3	6	5.5
Russia	3	2.5	15	0.3	9	0.2	0	0.0
UK	3	2.5	1072	24.1	354	6.5	9	8.3
USA	20	17.0	1003	22.4	1481	27.4	18	16.5
Total	119	100.0	4481	100.0*	5406	100.0	109	100.0

Missing data excluded here; percentage does not equal 100.

relative to that of the UK and European Union (EU) (Brenner, 2011). Though these conditions may make it easier for criminals to obtain data, they do not make it easier for individual buyers to utilize the data to their advantage. For example, if a buyer in Romania attempts to use US dump data to make purchases locally, it may be more likely to be flagged and the account closed than if the buyer were using a European card. Thus, the forums communicating in Russian languages may sell a higher proportion of European data in this sample than in the previous research on English-language groups.

To further explore pricing differences on the basis of the country of origin for stolen data, the logged mean price for bank accounts, CVVs, dumps, and fullz were compared by country (see Table 2.7). A log measure of price was used to normalize the variations in price for each product. As can be seen from the previous tables, there is a substantial range in prices for data, and logarithmic transformation minimizes the degree of variation. Binary measures were computed for each geographic category, such that any data from the USA was coded as 1, while all others were coded as 0. This enabled a comparison between the average logged price for the US data against the rest of the world in this sample to identify statistically significant differences. Groups were created for each region, and then analyzed using a t-test with unequal variances. A significant T value is an indication that there is a difference in the log price by region.

The results suggest that the mean price for data originating from the USA and UK are relatively inexpensive compared to other nations. The

Table 2.7 Location of data by mean log price

	Bank accounts			CVV			Dumps			Fullz		
	0	1	T	0	1	T	0	1	T	0	1	T
Asia	4.82	4.48	0.54	2.38	2.80	−5.36***	3.57	4.32	−12.31***	4.02	3.92	0.36
Australia and New Zealand	0	0	0	2.38	2.59	−3.40***	3.64	3.29	3.21***	4.00	4.08	−0.28
Canada	4.74	5.25	−1.06	2.39	2.38	0.32	3.67	3.37	5.90***	4.04	3.66	1.31
Europe	4.95	4.12	2.22*	2.16	2.98	26.19***	3.49	4.02	−14.17***	3.68	4.64	−6.83***
Other	4.76	5.09	−0.63	2.37	2.89	−6.14***	3.52	4.48	−19.09***	3.98	4.41	−1.31
Russia	0	0	0	2.39	3.49	−3.82***	3.64	3.85	−0.50	0	0	0
UK	4.82	4.08	0.85	2.40	2.37	0.99	3.69	2.81	13.00***	4.03	3.34	1.53
USA	4.68	5.33	−1.37	2.63	1.67	29.86***	3.85	3.04	22.05***	4.10	3.47	2.82**

Notes: The binary measures were computed for each geographic category. That is, bank accounts sold in Asia (1) compared to all other accounts (0), and the T indicates the t-test measure.
* $p \leq 0.05$, ** $p \leq 0.01$, *** $p \leq 0.001$; 0 = all other nations, 1 = selected country.

USA was the least expensive country for CVVs, as the average logged price was $1.67, compared to an average logged price from all other regions at $2.63. The US data was second to the UK originating data in terms of the price of dumps and fullz. This may be a consequence of the availability of data from the USA and UK saturating the market and reducing the overall advertised price (see also Herley & Florencio, 2010; Holt & Lampke, 2010). Dumps and fullz from Europe, Asia, and other nations, such as the Middle East, were the most expensive overall.

Bank account data from Europe is the least expensive, and statistically significant. Since the comparative category for each of our groups represents the rest of the world, it is interesting that only the European data is the least expensive and significant. There is no immediate explanation as to why this price differential exists, though it may be that individuals residing in Europe and Russia may be more easily able to access these accounts electronically. The mean price for data from both Canada and the UK were not significantly different, except in the case of dumps, where they were significantly lower than other nations. There is no immediate explanation for this variation, indicating the need for further research to explore the pricing structures of stolen data markets.

Summary

The forums in this sample provide access to a wide range of data and services to engage in fraud and theft. The majority of products sold involved dumps, CVVs, and other forms of personal data, while a smaller proportion of vendors offered services to obtain currency from stolen data. The ads also demonstrate the extent to which sellers cater to buyers, such as the use of customer service lines. Since the actual negotiation and purchase of data or services take place outside of the public setting of the forum, it is difficult to document the final price paid for services rendered. Using the information posted in the ads suggests that data is sold at a generally low price, making this a form of crime with a potentially high rate of return on an individual's investment. In addition, the price for data varied based on its country of origin, with the lowest prices in the USA, Europe, and the UK.

The range of ads posted across these forums makes it difficult for buyers to know who they should deal with in order to obtain valid data. As such, buyers are encouraged to provide feedback about their experiences so that others can identify trustworthy and reputable vendors. Negative feedback appeared in a number of threads. There is some variation in the nature of products sold in forums where there is a preponderance of negative complaints relative to those with generally positive feedback. As a consequence, there is a need to further explore how the presence of rippers affects the economy of these markets and how this may shape the creation of multiple markets separated on the basis of disreputable and legitimate vendors (see Herley & Florencio, 2010). We address these issues in Chap. 3 through various quantitative analyses.

References

Brenner, S. W. (2011). Defining cybercrime: A review of federal and state law. In R. D. Clifford (Ed.), *Cybercrime: The investigation, prosecution, and defense of a computer-related crime* (3rd ed., pp. 15–104). Raleigh, NC: Carolina Academic Press.

Chu, B., Holt, T. J., & Ahn, G. J. (2010). *Examining the creation, distribution, and function of malware on-line.* Technical Report for National Institute of Justice. NIJ Grant No. 2007-IJ-CX-0018. Retrieved from http://www.ncjrs.gov/pdffiles1/nij/grants/230112.pdf

Dhanjani, N., & Rios, B. (2008). *Bad sushi: Beating phishers at their own game.* Presented at the Annual Blackhat Meetings, Las Vegas, NV.

Franklin, J., Paxson, V., Perrig, A., & Savage, S. (2007). *An inquiry into the nature and cause of the wealth of internet miscreants.* Paper presented at CCS07, October 29–November 2, 2007, Alexandria, VA.

Herley, C., & Florencio, D. (2010). Nobody sells gold for the price of silver: Dishonesty, uncertainty and the underground economy. In T. Moor, D. J. Pym, & C. Ioannidis (Eds.), *Economics of information security and privacy* (pp. 35–53). New York: Springer.

Holt, T. J. (2013). Exploring the social organization and structure of stolen data markets. *Global Crime, 14,* 155–174.

Holt, T. J., & Lampke, E. (2010). Exploring stolen data markets on-line: Products and market forces. *Criminal Justice Studies, 23,* 33–50.

Holt, T. J., Smirnova, O., & Chua, Y.-T. (2013). An exploration of the factors affecting the advertised price for stolen data. *eCrime Researchers Summit (eCRS), 2013,* pp. 1–10. IEEE.

Holt, T. J., Strumsky, D., Smirnova, O., & Kilger, M. (2012). Examining the social networks of malware writers and hackers. *International Journal of Cyber Criminology, 6,* 891–903.

Holz, T., Engelberth, M., & Freiling, F. (2009). Learning more about the underground economy: A case-study of keyloggers and dropzones. In M. Backes & P. Ning (Eds.), *Computer security—ESCORICS* (pp. 1–18). Berlin and Heidelberg: Springer.

Honeynet Research Alliance. (2003). Profile: Automated credit card fraud. *Know Your Enemy Paper* series. Retrieved from http://www.honeynet.org/papers/profiles/ccfraud.pdf

Motoyama, M., McCoy, D., Levchenko, K., Savage, S., & Voelker, G. M. (2011). An analysis of underground forums. *IMC'11*, 71–79.

Newman, G., & Clarke, R. (2003). *Superhighway robbery: Preventing e-commerce crime*. Cullompton: Willan Press.

Symantec Corporation. (2012). *Symantec Internet security threat report, Volume 17*. Retrieved from http://www.symantec.com/threatreport/

Thomas, R., & Martin, J. (2006). The underground economy: Priceless. *;login: The Usenix Magazine, 31*, 7–17.

Verision. (2012). *2012 data breach investigations report and executive summary*. Retrieved from http://www.verisionbusiness.com/resources/reports/rp_data-breach-investigations-report-2012_en_xg.pdf

Wehinger, F. (2011). The Dark Net: Self-regulation dynamics of illegal online markets for identities and related services. *Intelligence and Security Informatics Conference*, 209–213.

Whitty, M. T. (2013). Anatomy of the online dating romance scam. *Security Journal, 28*(4): 443–455.

Whitty, M. T., & Buchanan, T. (2012). The online romance scam: A serious cybercrime. *CyberPsychology, Behavior, and Social Networking, 15*(3), 181–183.

CHAPTER 3

The Economic Impact of Stolen Data Markets

Abstract This chapter provides an in-depth analysis of the factors that may affect the price and profits received by data buyers and vendors within the market for stolen data. First, the issue of "lemon markets" is discussed, where the lack of information on the quality of data may lead to lower-priced data of low value dominating the market. Using linear regression models, we find that the price for dumps and eBay accounts are directly affected by social factors including the language of participants which may be a proxy for trust. Additionally, we discuss the challenges inherent in modeling the profit margins of data buyers and sellers. The prospective earnings of vendors are explored, suggesting they may make thousands of dollars depending on the product, while buyers could earn millions but face greater risk of economic loss.

Keywords Profits • Lemon market • Ripping • Language • Dumps

Thus far, we have demonstrated the range of products and services available in the market for stolen data and the potential variations present in the pricing of these resources. There are several potential explanations for the substantive differences in the price points for personal information, some of which may be driven by availability and quality. There is not a clear explanation, however, for potential variations in the price of information across all the forums sampled. It may be that market forces shape the potential tolerance that buyers may have for price variation, and that some markets may be generally less reliable than others which may lead to greater differences in price points. The ranges noted also make it difficult to discern how much profit buyers and sellers may gain through the sale and use of personal information. Since transactions are completed outside of the forums, there is no way to know the total number of exchanges between participants to demonstrate the scope of the market.

This chapter will address these two questions using quantitative analyses of the markets. We will first examine theoretical arguments regarding the economics of cybercrime, and its analogues to the economy for illicit goods in the real world. This will be followed by an exploration of the factors associated with the advertised price for dumps and eBay/PayPal accounts in these forums. We then present models to estimate the profits acquired by data sellers and buyers using information derived from positive and negative feedback provided. These models are then run to demonstrate the potential profits generated for dumps, CVVs, and eBay and PayPal accounts. The chapter concludes with a discussion of what these estimates can tell us about the economic impact of stolen data markets on consumers and financial institutions, as well as the implications for the profits generated from cybercrime generally.

Research on the Economics of Cybercrime

Before considering the economics of the market for stolen data, we must first consider what we understand about the general economic impact of cybercrime. Current statistics primarily estimate the cost of cybercrime, or its impact on victim communities, including industry and the general public (Cashell, Jackson, Jickling, & Webel, 2004; McAfee, 2013, 2014; Symantec Corporation, 2012). For example, Symantec estimated that the total cost due to cybercrime in the USA was $20.7 billion dollars in 2012 alone, with an average of $290 per victim (Symantec Corporation, 2012). Globally, the estimated cost of cybercrime ranges from around $226 billion to $575 billion depending on the data source (Cashell et al., 2004; McAfee, 2014).

There is, however, very little detail on the costs of cybercrime derived from data sources that can be accessed and analyzed by the academic community or general public. Most companies are reluctant to disclose data breaches and compromises, making it difficult to know the true scope of harm experienced by companies and individuals (Cashell et al.,

2004; McAfee, 2013; Moore, Clayton, & Anderson, 2009; Ponemon Institute, 2014). A small number of security firms produce yearly statistics on data breaches, though they intentionally exclude mass breaches so as to avoid potential skew in cost metrics (e.g. Ponemon Institute, 2014). Furthermore, their data is generated from interviews with security personnel within a sample of different organizations each year which may or may not have experienced an incident (Computer Security Institute, 2010; Ponemon Institute, 2014). Thus, the findings do not reflect all breaches globally year over year.

Similarly, it is extremely difficult to quantify losses, as there are direct and indirect costs which must be calculated, some of which cannot be assigned a value or be consistently calculated (Moore et al., 2009; Ponemon Institute, 2014). For instance, the Ponemon institute asks respondents to provide data on the direct and indirect costs their organization incurs due to a data breach. Their direct measures involve costs from external service providers, while indirect costs are based on internal investigation expenses and the organization's expected customer loss estimates. Though external costs can be validated against cost metrics from service providers, the indirect cost of time and productivity may be more esoteric (Moore et al., 2009). Furthermore, these estimates provide no measurement for the costs experienced by individual consumers who lose data in a breach. Thus these figures cannot be extended to the individual victims, only the organizations impacted.

There is also generally little research considering how much offenders may stand to gain from their involvement in cybercrimes. It is assumed that cybercrimes involve a low probability of arrest, and high-yield returns from trading compromised data for money (Kshetri, 2006; Moore et al., 2009). Personal financial information has its own inherent value based on the amount of money available in the case of checking or savings accounts, or the total balance limit for credit cards. Thus, there should be some way to quantify the profit motives behind fraud and data theft.

The current literature does not emphasize, however, the economic incentives inherent in some forms of cybercrime. For instance, Franklin, Paxson, Perrig, and Savage (2007) estimated the total wealth generated from an underground market found on IRC by examining the types and amount of products. They found potential profits for participants totaled over $37,000,000 based on the amount of data sold and the estimated average loss for credit and debit card fraud (Franklin et al., 2007).

Similarly, Stone-Gross and colleagues (2011) estimated that three groups selling fake antivirus software made an estimated $130 million in profits.

The absence of information may stem from the complex pricing structures observed for information and services offered in data and cybercrime markets. As noted in Chap. 2, an individual seller may offer multiple types of dumps from different countries with tiered pricing based in part on location, card issuer, and available balance (Franklin et al., 2007; Herley & Florencio, 2010; Holt & Lampke, 2010). Additionally, some sellers offered discounted pricing schemes based on the quantity of data purchased, making it difficult to disaggregate the individual price for each item (Franklin et al., 2007; Holt & Lampke, 2010). Finally, the negotiation process and purchase of data takes place outside of the forum or public component of the IRC channel, making it extremely difficult to know the quantity of data purchased or the final price paid for information (Franklin et al., 2007; Herley & Florencio, 2010; Holt & Lampke, 2010; Motoyama, McCoy, Levchenko, Savage, & Voelker, 2011; Wehinger, 2011).

Despite these issues, it is important to recognize that the advertised price for data may be an important indication of seller reputation and their potential to offer valid products. Specifically, Herley and Florencio (2010) argue that the pricing of data is a key marker of the legitimacy of the market as a whole. Individuals who sell data at dramatically discounted prices may be rippers attempting to entice unskilled or new buyers to purchase their data. The individuals who buy this information may not receive any data at all, or be given invalid card details. The lack of information available about the quality of products relative to their price creates a "lemon market" for data (Akerlov, 1970), as buyers are unable to differentiate low- and high-quality resources and may tend to go with the lowest-priced information first. As a result, quality sellers cannot compete and are driven on to other environments, leaving buyers with access to bad data (Herley & Florencio, 2010). As a result, the initial low prices they may pay are obviated through repeat purchasing from other vendors in order to finally acquire workable data.

There is, however, a second market operating with greater degrees of trust between participants which are structured to minimize the risk of loss. The advertised price for data may appear higher within these markets, though purchasing this data will likely lead to working information that can be used to engage in fraud and theft (see Herley & Florencio, 2010; Holt et al., 2013). Though the initial investment costs for buyers will be high, it will be lower in the long term because they will only have to purchase data one time to acquire functional information rather than make multiple lower-priced purchases (Herley & Florencio, 2010).

If there is a relationship between the price of data and the reliability of a market, then it is possible that certain factors present in the language of advertisements that are associated with the advertised price. As noted in Chap. 2, there are various market conditions that structure the relationships between buyers and sellers and demonstrate who may be more reliable than others. For instance, those sellers who offer customer service may attract customers because they may offer aid in the event data is not functional (Holt & Lampke, 2010). Similarly, sellers who offer free replacements for invalid data may be able to draw in new customers who are unfamiliar with how to make the data more effective (Herley & Florencio, 2010; Holt & Lampke, 2010). The presence of rippers may also be associated with lower pricing because of the potential to be cheated by disreputable vendors offering low-quality information.

Thus, it is possible that there may be a link between the practices of sellers, the market conditions generally, and the pricing for data offered in a given forum. If lemon markets for stolen data exist (Herley & Florencio, 2010), then it is likely that they will have the lowest general pricing relative to more organized and trustworthy markets. There is, however, minimal empirical research assessing the relationship between the operational functions of a forum and the price for data. There is even less research examining prospective differences in the profits obtained by sellers and buyers dependent on the forums in which they operate. Given the interrelated nature of these questions, we will consider each of these questions in turn.

Assessing the Forces Shaping Market Pricing

In order to explore the influence of social and market forces on the advertised price for data, the factors affecting the advertised prices for dumps and eBay/PayPal account credentials were examined using linear regression techniques. We will explore the relationship between the language in ads, the market conditions, and the advertised price for data to explore the potential for there to be multiple markets operating for data within this sample of forums (Herley & Florencio, 2010; Wehinger, 2011). We will focus our analysis on the factors affecting the advertised prices for dumps and eBay/PayPal account credentials using linear regression techniques.

As noted in Chap. 2, dumps were the most common item sold, though eBay and PayPal accounts were less common. We examine both to provide a point of comparison between these products available in the market.

In order to capture the price for data, we used the log advertised price observed for both products. Using the log price helps minimize the skew observed in pricing (Oliver & Norberg, 2010), which ranged from $0.04 to $8000 for dumps and $0.40 to $800.00 for eBay data. In addition, 570 dump ads were removed ($N=5167$), and 65 eBay and PayPal ads ($N=118$) due to missing price information.

To identify what factors may be associated with data pricing and, therefore, reflect a lemon market for information, we included multiple social and market-related variables. First, we created four binary measures (0 = no; 1 = yes) for the payment method a seller accepted: *Western Union*, *WebMoney*, *Liberty Reserve*, and *Escrow* payments. Sellers who accepted Western Union payments may have higher prices because of the difficulty associated with accepting paper currency at a physical location (Herley & Florencio, 2010; Holt & Lampke, 2010; Wehinger, 2011). In addition, accepting Western Union payments may be an indication of actor sophistication as they must work in cooperation with others in order to acquire, transfer, and accept payments (Herley & Florencio, 2010; Holt, 2013; Wehinger, 2011). The use of escrow payments may also be associated with higher prices because escrow payments depend on the use of a trusted intermediary actor to ensure the likelihood of a successful transaction. The reduced risk of loss afforded by escrow payments may increase the legitimacy of the market and trust between participants (e.g. Holt, 2013).

Electronic payment methods like WebMoney and Liberty Reserve may, however, be associated with lower prices because they allow immediate money transfers between the buyer and seller (Motoyama et al., 2011). Though electronic currency payments are the historical standard in data markets (e.g. Franklin et al., 2007; Holt & Lampke, 2010), they may be more attractive to rippers as they ensure immediate payment and do not require an immediate reciprocal exchange for data to be made.

Four binary measures (0 = no; 1 = yes) for customer service were also included to understand any relationship they may have to the advertised price for products. First, *customer service* was included based on the sellers' indicating they operated dedicated lines of communication for customer support via ICQ or email in case of questions or issues (Holt & Lampke, 2010; Wehinger, 2011). This variable also measures whether the seller specified that they would provide support for buyers after a purchase in order to facilitate the use of data. Either form of support may be associated with higher pricing because of the perceived legitimacy of the seller and their reputation (Holt & Lampke, 2010; Wehinger, 2011). This measure was not included in the model for eBay and PayPal credentials due to missing data.

Second, a measure was included for *tests or free samples* of data on the basis of sellers providing them in an ad in order to attract customers. Since credit or debit card data has intrinsic value to both a buyer and seller, posting this information at no charge may be a way for a seller to validate their products (Dhanjani & Rios, 2008; Franklin et al., 2007; Holt & Lampke, 2010). At the same time, it is likely a way for unscrupulous vendors to rip off unsuspecting customers by attracting them with the promise of valid data (Herley & Florencio, 2010; Wehinger, 2011). Those sellers who do not give away such data may be more trustworthy as they do not degrade their profit margins by giving information away to others (Herley & Florencio, 2010). Thus, the use of free samples should correspond to lower advertised prices as a reflection of a lemon market for data (Herley & Florencio, 2010).

The third measure of customer service measured was free *replacements* for invalid or expired accounts. Sellers indicated that they would replace accounts that were inactive within a certain time period after purchase in order to satisfy customers after a purchase (Franklin et al., 2007; Holt & Lampke, 2010). Though it may be helpful for the client, the free release of data limits sellers' profit margins (Herley & Florencio, 2010). As a result, there may be an association between lower pricing for data and the use of free replacements by sellers. This may serve as a potential marker of lemon markets, though it may also be a genuine attempt on the part of some sellers to attract customers (Herley & Florencio, 2010).

The final measure of customer service is a binary measure capturing whether or not a seller has had their *product tested* by the forum moderators. Since more reliable forums operate testing services for sellers to have their products validated and publicly reviewed, those who go through the process can be trusted (Holt, 2013; Holt & Lampke, 2010; Wehinger, 2011). Testing services are not present in all forums, and serve as an important marker for trust, but not a guarantee of seller's reputation. There is an expectation, however, that testing services may increase prices because they minimize the risks for participants (Herley & Florencio, 2010; Wehinger, 2011).

Two variables were also included to assess the influence of customer comments on the pricing for data. Specifically, two continuous variables were created based on the number of *positive* and *negative feedback* posted about a seller's products within any given thread. Feedback enables buyers to publicly describe their experiences with sellers, and document the quality of the product and the seller's behaviors (Holt, 2013; Holt & Lampke, 2010; Motoyama et al., 2011 Wehinger, 2011). Positive feedback may draw other potential customers to a seller, while negative feedback may harm a seller's reputation, particularly if data was not delivered or was of low quality or value. It is possible that individuals may post false feedback in an attempt to either harm a competitor or generate interest in their products (Herley & Florencio, 2010; Holt, 2013). There may also be no feedback in a thread because the ad may have been posted recently or reflect a general lack of interest in a given product within the market. Thus, feedback serves as a potential barometer for the legitimacy of a market. Both measures are included in the model for dumps, though only positive feedback is used in the eBay and PayPal credential model due to multicollinearity issues.

An additional continuous variable was also created to assess the number of instances of *hijacking*, where individuals place an ad for their products in an existing sellers' thread. Attempts at hijacking may serve as an indicator of a lemon market, as this practice disadvantages the TS and creates direct competition (Wehinger, 2011). Better organized forums with substantial management and oversight by moderators do not allow such practices and can ban a user for this activity (Holt, 2013). Thus, the presence of hijackers in a thread should be correlated with reduced prices for stolen data.

An additional binary measure was created to examine the relationship between product pricing and the proportion of *ripping* complaints received within a forum (0 = no; 1 = yes) (Herley & Florencio, 2010). As noted in Chap. 2, three of the forums in our sample received a large number of ripping complaints overall. Since two of the forums had over 30 % of threads containing complaints, we chose to code these two forums as ripping forums (1 = Yes) to control for the potential that these forums were infiltrated by rippers, creating a potential lemon market, while the remainder were coded as non-ripping (0 = No). It is expected that prices in the ripping forums will have lower advertised prices to attract participants, relative to the larger sample of non-ripping markets (Holt & Lampke, 2010). This measure was, however, excluded in the model for eBay and

PayPal data due to the small proportion of these data advertised in ripping forums (22%) and multicollinearity issues.

A final binary variable was included for the primary language used by forum participants (0-Eng; 1-Rus). English speakers who do not have any familiarity with Russian will have difficulty communicating or participating in the market. Rippers might be attracted to English-language forums because it increases their pool of buyers globally, including access to inexperienced buyers. In addition, participants in the three forums with the greatest proportion of complaints communicated primarily in English. Russian-language forums might also have lower prices because of market insulation and increased trust between participants (Herley & Florencio, 2010; Holt & Lampke, 2010; Wehinger, 2011). Thus, language was included as a potential measure for lemon markets.

The results of the regression model for the advertised price for dumps demonstrated that there are several factors associated with the advertised price for data (see Table 3.1, Model 1). Those who accepted Western Union and escrow payments advertised dumps at higher prices than other sellers in keeping with the hypothesis that these payment systems are associated with legitimate markets due to the need for trust and insularity between market actors. The use of the electronic currency WebMoney was associated with lower pricing, though Liberty Reserve was associated with higher pricing.

Several markers of customer service were also associated with higher prices indicating these factors may serve as markets for trust. Sellers who offered a customer service or support line had higher prices, as did those whose products had been tested. The use of free replacements was associated with lower prices as hypothesized, suggesting it is an indication of a seller's involvement in a lemon market (Herley & Florencio, 2010). Thus, vendors interested in ripping off their clients may offer free replacements as a mechanism to entice prospective buyers into purchasing data.

Several of the market factors were also associated with lower pricing overall. Positive feedback from buyers was associated with a 3% decrease in the price for data, as was the presence of hijackers in a forum. The products sold in ripping forums were also 44% lower in price than those in non-ripping forums as hypothesized. Russian-language forums had lower pricing for dumps than those in English-language forums, which may be a reflection of insularity in market pricing due to language barriers for non-native speakers and a greater presence of Russian cybercriminals who operate within this space (see Holt, 2013).

Table 3.1 Regression models of log price for dumps and eBay/PayPal credentials

	Model 1: Dumps (N=5167)				Model 2: eBay/PayPal (N=118)			
Variables	B	S.E.	Beta	% change[a]	B	S.E.	Beta	% change
Western Union	0.562	0.044	0.228***	75.5	1.546	0.402	0.344***	369.3
WebMoney	-0.313	0.043	-0.111***	-26.9	1.837	0.492	0.430***	527.8
Liberty Reserve	0.178	0.044	0.044***	19.5	-2.170	0.571	-0.442***	-88.6
Escrow payment	1.381	0.077	0.282***	298.0	-1.181	1.068	-0.124	–
Customer service	0.096	0.049	0.028*	10.1	–	–	–	–
Test/free samples	-0.085	0.086	-0.013	–	0.493	0.627	0.072	–
Free replacements	-0.409	0.038	-0.168***	-33.5	2.294	1.021	0.241	891.9
Product tested	0.700	0.081	0.122***	101.3	-0.624	3.436	-0.054	–
Positive comments	-0.033	0.006	-0.095***	-3.3	2.776	0.636	0.407***	1505.6
Negative comments	-0.026	0.014	-0.034	–	1.568	0.907	0.555	–
Hijackers	-0.111	0.045	-0.034*	-10.5	-0.419	0.250	-0.181	–
Ripper forum	-0.583	0.050	-0.239	-44.2	–	–	–	–
Russian	-0.828	0.094	-0.130***	-56.3	-1.498	0.309	-0.479**	-77.7
Intercept	3.892	0.063***			2.712	0.288***		

Model 1: $F=108.949***$; 0.000, $R^2=0.216$, Adjusted $R^2=0.214$
Model 2: $F=16.202***$, 0.000, $R^2=0.627$, Adjusted $R^2=0.588$
*$p\leq 0.05$; **$p\leq 0.01$; ***$p\leq 0.001$

[a] When the dependent variable is logged transformed, as with prices in our models, then we can interpret coefficients as percent changes when we take the exponent of the regression coefficient

An additional regression model was created to assess the factors affecting the log advertised price for eBay and PayPal credentials (see Table 3.1, Model 2). There were some pertinent differences between the price for this type of data and dumps, which may stem from the smaller number of eBay and PayPal data sold in this sample of forums. For instance, sellers who accepted Liberty Reserve and escrow payments had significantly lower advertised prices. By contrast, Western Union payments were associated with higher advertised prices, as were WebMoney payments. Sellers who received positive feedback had generally much higher prices for their products. Hijackers were associated with 43% lower advertised prices, as were products advertised in Russian-language forums which were 78% lower overall.

Though these product types are not perfect points of comparison, there are some consistent relationships that support the potential for lemon markets and insular markets for data generally. The association between the presence of positive feedback and hijackers may reflect the importance of market actors' behavior generally. Forums that do not regulate the practices of sellers, enabling hijacking, may be more likely to involve rippers and generally higher degrees of risk. The association between language is also pertinent as products offered in Russian-language forums had lower prices overall. Though we assume that lower pricing is generally a reflection of a lemon market for data, the language used by actors may serve as a point of insulation that can reduce the likelihood of penetration by unfamiliar actors. In this case, English-language hackers who want to gain access to carding markets may be less capable of participating in Russian markets. Thus, language may actually help keep pricing down because the Russian-language market may be flooded with stolen data goods that the hackers cannot cash out on time. These preliminary findings thus give initial support to the supposition that there are different markets based on insularity and the presence of prospective rippers (Herley & Florencio, 2010; Wehinger, 2011).

Estimating the Economy of Stolen Data Markets

If there are multiple markets operating for data with different pricing, it is important to consider how much profit individual participants may be able to generate from a sale. There are, however, virtually no estimates of the total economy of stolen data markets using actual pricing from advertisers (see Holt & Lampke, 2010; Holt et al., 2014). The lack of information may be a consequence of the limited data available on the total number of completed transactions between buyers and sellers in these markets. Since purchases and exchanges take place via private communications between the buyer and the seller, there are few sources available to validate how many purchases are completed. Furthermore, there is little information on the final price paid for data, or the quantities traded, and it is difficult to estimate the profits of data sellers or the potential margins for buyers (Holt, 2013; Holt & Lampke, 2010; Motoyama et al., 2011). Estimating buyers' profits are especially challenging as they may experience unsuccessful transactions due to purchasing data from rippers. At the same time, a buyer may purchase data from a legitimate seller whose information has been deactivated due to card discovery and account closure (Peretti, 2009). Thus, researchers must attempt to find ways to control for buyers' potential failure to monetize data purchased from a seller.

One way to do this may be to use feedback as a proxy for the number of times a buyer and seller engage in a transaction to know whether they were able to use the data they bought, or simply lost money from the transaction. As noted previously in this chapter, customers in data markets are encouraged and expected to publicly post their experiences with a seller in their thread to describe their encounters (Holt & Lampke, 2010; Motoyama et al., 2011; Wehinger, 2011). If a customer did not feel satisfied, then they should provide negative feedback regarding their experience with the seller. The same is true for successful encounters which should generate positive feedback about the seller's practices or data (Herley & Florencio, 2010; Holt, 2013; Holt & Lampke, 2010; Motoyama et al., 2011).

The use of feedback gives a prospective measure of the total number of publicly acknowledged transactions attempted between buyers and sellers (Holt, 2013; Holt & Lampke, 2010; Motoyama et al., 2011; Wehinger, 2011). We may be able to estimate the profits made by each side of a transaction on the basis of whether the feedback provided was positive or negative. Essentially, the nature of the feedback can reveal whether the data buyer was able to successfully acquire funds from reliable products and/or active data (see Fig. 3.1). Sellers are able to make a profit regardless of whether their data is useable, though positive feedback will most likely be provided to those whose customers are satisfied with their experience. Vendors who sell false information, or provide no data at all, are more likely to receive negative feedback.

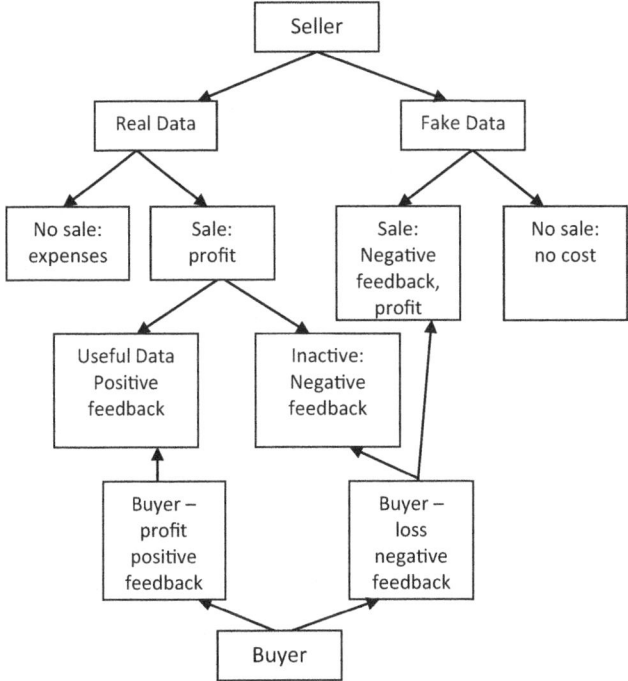

Fig. 3.1 The process of data sales within on-line markets

Buyers will only be able to obtain funds from account data that is active and valid. Paying for inactive information or receiving nothing from a vendor leads to an immediate loss that cannot be recovered. Engaging in a transaction with a vendor with positive feedback does not guarantee, however, that all accounts will be active and valid at the time of purchase. Financial institutions are increasingly alerting customers when their information may have been lost through a breach, and may reissue cards to reduce the ability of criminals to use the information (Peretti, 2009; Seals, 2014). Vendors may not be able to test all the data they have for sale, leading to the potential that buyers may receive inactive accounts.

As a result, it is difficult to assume that all data purchased from a vendor is able to generate success for buyers regardless of the vendors' intent. Negative feedback is a demonstration that a buyer was unable to gain a profit from their purchase, while positive feedback suggests some of the data may have been useable. As a result, it becomes important to estimate the conditional buyers' profits since they may stimulate demand for data and more accurately reflects the likelihood that some, but not all, of the information could be manipulated for a profit.

In addition, examining profit levels on the basis of positive and negative feedback may further our understanding of the concept of lemon markets for stolen data. Since there are observed differences in the price of data based on the social and market conditions of a forum, it is plausible that there may be differences in the profits obtained by both buyers and sellers depending on the forum. Those forums with a higher preponderance of ripping complaints may have generally smaller profits for buyers due to the risk of loss, while more legitimate forums may lead to greater buyer profits. If this relationship can be quantified, then we may be able to find further support for Herley and Florencio's (2010) arguments on the existence of the two-tiered stolen data markets. Thus, we attempted to examine these issues using feedback as a measure of completed transactions within each forum.

Estimating the Profits of Data Sellers and Buyers

To assess the prospective profits generated by participants within this sample of forums, we chose to focus on three of the most common products: (1) dumps, (2) CVVs, and (3) eBay and PayPal accounts. We considered the total number of feedback posts provided as a proxy for the total number of transactions that occurred in these forums. We also segmented the transactions on the basis of whether they occurred in ripping and non-ripping forums to examine any variations in the pricing structures for products and the proportion of feedback received (see Herley & Florencio, 2010; Holt et al., 2013).

In all, there were 190 transactions in the non-ripping forums and 67 in the ripping forum sample for dumps (see Table 3.2 for descriptives). Within those non-ripping forums, 62% of the reported feedback was positive ($N=117$), compared to 36% ($N=24$) in the ripping forums. CVVs data sellers received only two instances of feedback in the non-ripping forums, all of which were negative. There were, however, 61 instances of feedback observed in ripping forums for CVVs data sellers, and 40% of those ($N=25$) involved positive feedback. For eBay/PayPal accounts, there were six pieces of feedback observed in the non-ripping forums, and

Table 3.2 Total potential transactions

Product type	Non-ripping	Ripping	Total
CVV	2	61	63
Dumps	190	67	257
eBay/PayPal	6	3	9
Total	198	131	329

Note: The total feedback may indicate the number of total sales from the sellers, and be a good proxy for their profits

three in the ripping forums. As a result, there appears to be some difference in the proportion of products sold within each forum type.

To estimate the revenue of data sellers we used the following formula:

Total Seller's Revenue = total feedback × advertised price × lot size × probability of success

Using positive and negative feedback enabled the identification of all potential transactions regardless of the utility of the data for the buyer. We also used the minimum, maximum, mean, and median advertised prices for data. Since sellers posted advertised prices for data sold in the market, all four figures are used to demonstrate the potential range of profits generated by sellers. Additionally, the currency used by all vendors was converted into US dollars, the most common form of currency used, to create a consistent data point (Franklin et al., 2007; Holt & Lampke, 2010; Holt, 2013; Holt & Smirnova, 2014; Motoyama et al., 2011; Yip et al., 2013).

This figure was then multiplied by the size of the lot of data that may have been purchased. As noted earlier, data was typically priced based on an individual unit or card, but were sold in quantities or lots which varied in size based on vendors and product types. For instance, many dumps vendors indicated that they prefer buyers to purchase data in quantities of 100 or more accounts at a time (e.g. Franklin et al., 2007; Herley & Florencio, 2010; Holt & Lampke, 2010). All the data for these calculations was generated from the forum posts so as to reflect the conditions of the market rather than speculative pricing from other sources.

Thus, the quantity of data sold per lot was used to more accurately capture the prospective revenue of sellers. The transactions may have lots of various sizes starting with 25, and up to 100. Seller revenues are estimated based on the number of transactions (e.g. 190 for dumps in non-ripping forums), multiplied by the number of potential lot sizes (ranging from 25 to 100) multiplied by the price per item (ranging from minimum to maximum prices).

Finally, this number is then adjusted by the probability of accuracy in the feedback provided for a successful transaction. A buyer may choose not to provide feedback so as to minimize their on-line presence and hide their overt involvement in cybercrime markets. Others may simply opt not to participate in the collegial nature of the marketplace (Holt, 2013). Some feedback may also be falsified in order to increase the perceived reliability of a vendor in the market. An unscrupulous seller may create multiple user profiles and post fictitious reviews indicating that they successfully completed a transaction in order to drive real customers to the vendor (e.g. Holt et al., 2015).

To control for the possibility of measurement error based on false or missing feedback, it is necessary to control for the probability of actual transactions completed. Since it is impossible to know the accuracy of feedback provided, an alternative solution would be to condition the outcomes by quartiles in order to provide estimates for situations where feedback does not represent correct transactions due to various factors to avoid overestimation. For instance, the use of a 25% increment is intended to reflect seller profits in the event that the majority (or 75%) of feedback posted was faked and only 25% may represent the results of actual transactions. We increase the probabilities of accurate feedback up to 100% accuracy where all feedback received is assumed to be correct. With each incremental increase, profit margins for seller increase as well. That is, the more accurate the feedback, the money the sellers may have made. Alternatively, a large fraction of false feedback reduces sellers' earnings.

This formula limits the measurable number of transactions that occurred with these forums. Vendors who received no feedback are excluded from this analysis, which does not necessarily mean they did not have buyers for their products. They may have recently posted their ad, had minimal customer interest in their products, or experienced private contacts outside of the forum that were otherwise undocumented in the threads (see Motoyama et al., 2011). Since there is no way to control this issue, we must caution readers to interpret our findings not as concrete metrics for profit but as potential estimates for profits that have a substantive margin of error.

A similar formula can be used to assess the revenues generated by buyers within stolen data markets:

Total Buyer Profits = (positive feedback × lot size × identity theft losses × probability of success)
−advertised price of data

We used only positive feedback as they signal that an individual was able to utilize the data they purchased (see Table 3.3 for distribution of positive feedback by product type and forum type). Due to the limited number of positive feedback instances reported for CVV and eBay/PayPal data, buyer revenue estimates will only be generated for dump data. The presence of positive feedback in non-ripping forums indicates that 62% of sales led to successful buyer transactions from the purchase of dumps, and only 17% from eBay/PayPal transactions. The ripping forums, however, had a slightly lower proportion of positive feedback for both product types (approximately 41% for all products).

The total number of positive feedback responses posted was then multiplied by the size of the lot, as a basis for the total number of pieces purchased. There is, however, no easy way to determine how much money may have been earned from each dump purchased. One potential data source to determine prospective buyer profits is to use loss estimates for identity theft due to credit or bank account fraud since this is the most likely outcome from the purchase of dumps. Thus, we used estimates for both credit card and bank account fraud generated from the National Crime Victimization Survey (NCVS) Identity Theft Supplement of 2012 (Harrell & Langton, 2013). This study measures the financial losses of victims aged 16 and older who experienced at least one attempted or successful identity theft incident over a 12-month period from 2011 to 2012. The report (Harrell & Langton, 2013) provides a range of financial losses reported by victims. We used the mean and median direct losses for exist-

Table 3.3 Total successful transactions for buyers

Product type	Non-ripping	Ripping	Total
CVV	0	25	25
Dumps	117	24	141
eBay/PayPal	1	1	2
Total	118	50	168

Note: The positive comments indicate the number of transactions that the buyers may be satisfied with

ing credit cards ($1448; $300) and bank accounts ($551; $200) from the NCVS report to calculate buyers' profits. These figures provide a more conservative estimate for victim losses rather than indirect out-of-pocket costs which may have been reimbursed to victims by insurance companies or financial institutions (Harrell & Langton, 2013).

The use of identity theft loss statistics are limited since they do not disaggregate high- and low-tech identity theft victimization (Harrell & Langton, 2013). There are, however, few other consistently reported and widely cited data points that may be used to access economic cybercrimes. For instance, the Ponemon Institute (2014) provides yearly statistics on data breaches reported by a sample of businesses and industry, along with the prospective dollar loss suffered by individual victims of a breach. Few corporations and businesses report their losses in this report, and their data excludes major breaches which would affect large populations, such as the Target breach (Ponemon, 2014). Victims of those breaches still experience economic loss which means their estimates may underrepresent the amount of injury caused by the loss of financial information. As a result, the NCVS statistics may be a more accurate reflection of the profits generated by data thieves who use credit card or bank account information, and their prospective return on investment. Therefore, the buyers' profits estimates combine the data collected from the NCVS on identity theft losses as the proxy for buyers' revenues and the data collected on prices, lots, and transactions from the forum threads.

This figure was then multiplied by the probability of successful transactions (25, 50, 75, and 100%) to adjust for the likelihood of successful data manipulation, such as false feedback posted by a vendor (Herley & Florencio, 2010). Finally, the advertised price for stolen data was subtracted from this amount as a proxy for buyers' cost estimates. Even though we do not have the costs of labor and other components of buyers' expenditures, their expenses should equal to at least the prices that they have paid to acquire the data. This estimate provides a potential return on investment over and above their initial purchase costs.

The resulting figure does not factor in the total number of man-hours required to complete a successful data breach to acquire economic information due to variations in the actors' skill and technical expertise, along with the complexity of the attack vector and target security (see Holt & Kilger, 2012). Similarly, the time and costs a buyer incurs to acquire funds may differ based on the quality of the data and their use of money laundering services (e.g. Herley & Florencio, 2010; Holt & Lampke, 2010).

Thus, these costs were not included in these economic estimates due to the difficulty in computing these figures. The findings do, however, provide a valuable baseline to assess the initial size of the economy based on direct exchanges between buyers and sellers.

ESTIMATING SELLER PROFITS

Using these formulae, we first examined the potential range of seller revenues in ripping and non-ripping forums for dumps, CVVs, and eBay/PayPal accounts, respectively. Tables 3.4 and 3.5 show the calculations for 50 and 100 unit lots for dumps and CVVs; Table 3.6 uses 25 and 50 unit lots as they were more frequent for eBay/PayPal data. Beginning with dumps, sellers appeared to generate very little revenue at the 25% probability level using minimum prices (see Table 3.4). Sellers potentially earned $1615 in non-ripping forums and $11.39 in ripping forums. This estimate changed substantially within both ripping and non-ripping forums using the median and average price for dump data. If only 25% of the transactions result in sales using the largest lot size and the median advertised price, dumps vendors may have earned $285,000 in non-ripping and $41,875 in ripping forums, respectively.

When combined, this suggests dumps vendors may have earned $326,875 over the lifetime of observed posts. This number suggests that dumps vendors may make some profit regardless of the utility of the data they sell (Herley & Florencio, 2010). In addition, the price difference noted between the forum types supports the assertion that there may be a lemon market for dumps, with more organized forums charging higher average prices with less variation in all prices (Herley & Florencio, 2010; Holt et al., 2013).

The estimated revenue for CVV data sellers were lower than that of dumps sellers which may be a function of the generally lower prices for this type of data (see Table 3.5). Using the minimum values suggests sales in ripping forums were profitable and plentiful, even at the 25% probability level. Using the mean and average prices for data suggests sellers may be able to earn up to $36,600 and $78,629 for lots of 50 in ripping forums. These prices are discernibly higher than those CVV prices in the non-ripping forums, where sellers may obtain revenues between $1000 and $3894. In addition, there were more instances of feedback posted in ripping forums, though only 39% of all feedback was positive.

Table 3.4 Seller revenue for dumps

Price	50 dump lot				100 dump lot			
	25%	50%	75%	100%	25%	50%	75%	100%
Non-ripping forums								
$2.00	$4750.00	$9500.00	$14,250.00	$19,000.00	$9500.00	$19,000.00	$28,500.00	$38,000.00
$60.00	$142,500.00	$285,000.00	$427,500.00	$570,000.00	$285,000.00	$570,000.00	$855,000.00	$1,140,000.00
$104.47	$248,116.30	$496,232.50	$744,348.75	$992,465.00	$496,232.50	$992,465.00	$1,488,697.50	$1,984,930.00
$7000.00	$16,625,000.00	$33,325,000.00	$49,875,000.00	$66,500,000.00	$33,250,000.00	$66,500,000.00	$99,750,000.00	$133,000,000.00
Ripping forums								
$0.04	$33.50	$67.00	$100.50	$134.00	$67.00	$134.00	$201.00	$268.00
$25.00	$20,937.50	$41,875.00	$62,812.50	$83,750.00	$41,875.00	$83,750.00	$125,625.00	$167,500.00
$101.34	$84,872.25	$169,744.50	$254,616.75	$339,489.00	$169,744.50	$339,489.00	$509,233.50	$6,789,780.00
$8000.00	$6,700,000	$13,400,000.00	$20,100,000.00	$26,800,000.00	$13,400,000.00	$26,800,000.00	$40,200,000.00	$53,600,000.00

Table 3.5 Estimated seller revenue for CVV data

Price	50 lot				100 lot			
	25%	50%	75%	100%	25%	50%	75%	100%
Non-ripping forums								
$2.00	50.00	100.00	150.00	200.00	100.00	200.00	300.00	400.00
$10.00	250.00	500.00	750.00	1000.00	500.00	1000.00	1500.00	2000.00
$38.94	973.50	1947.00	2920.50	3894.00	1947.00	3894.00	5841.00	7788.00
$200.00	5000.00	10,000.00	15,000.00	20,000.00	10,000.00	20,000.00	30,000.00	40,000.00
Ripping forums								
$1.00	762.50	1525.00	2287.50	3050.00	1525.00	3050.00	4575.00	6100.00
$12.00	9150.00	18,300.00	27,450.00	36,600.00	18,300.00	36,600.00	54,900.00	73,200.00
$25.78	19,657.30	39,314.50	58,971.80	78,629.00	39,314.50	78,629.00	117,943.50	157,258.00
$800.00	6,100,000.00	12,200,000.00	18,300,000.00	24,400,000.00	12,200,000.00	24,400,000.00	36,600,000.00	48,800,000.00

Table 3.6 Estimated seller revenue for eBay/PayPal account data

Price	25 lot				50 lot			
	25%	50%	75%	100%	25%	50%	75%	100%
Non-ripping forums								
$1.00	37.50	75.00	112.50	150.00	75.00	150.00	225.00	300.00
$4.00	150.00	300.00	450.00	600.00	300.00	600.00	900.00	1200.00
$12.13	454.90	909.80	1364.60	1819.50	909.80	1819.50	2729.30	3639.00
$150.00	5625.00	11,250.00	16,875.00	22,500.00	11,250.00	22,500.00	33,750.00	45,000.00
Ripping forums								
$0.20	3.75	7.50	11.250	15.00	7.5	15.00	22.50	30.00
$45.00	843.75	1687.50	2531.25	3375.00	1687.50	3375.00	5062.50	6750.00
$80.78	1514.63	3029.25	4543.88	6058.50	3029.25	6058.50	9087.75	12,117.00
$800.00	15,000.00	30,000.00	45,000.00	60,000.00	30,000.00	60,000.00	90,000.00	120,000.00

The variations observed may be an indication that CVV data are a valuable commodity that rippers can exploit to their advantage in lemon markets (Herley & Florencio, 2010). Specifically, CVV data enables buyers to immediately begin making purchases through on-line retailers and phone transactions and thereby profit from their purchase without the need for money launderers or other services (Holt & Lampke, 2010). This information may be particularly attractive to novices who seek to engage in fraud and theft but do not have all the skills needed to effectively engage in these offenses individually. Thus, unscrupulous sellers may easily attract buyers regardless of the pricing of their data (Herley & Florencio, 2010). The fact that there were no instances of positive feedback observed in the non-ripping forums further demonstrated that CVV data may be distinctly targeted to novices who may be willing to accept greater risk in order to obtain useful information (Herley & Florencio, 2010).

The same price differences were noted for eBay/PayPal accounts as ripping forums had lower median and average prices (see Table 3.6). There was a higher variance in prices within the ripping forums, indicating the risk of fraudulent transactions affected the price for data within the market as a whole (Herley & Florencio, 2010; Holt et al., 2013). Advertised prices were more consistent within non-ripping forums, suggesting that vendors may not generate as much revenue despite reporting a higher proportion of sales (Herley & Florencio, 2010). In fact, using the average price for eBay data from non-ripping forums at the 25- and 50-piece lot level demonstrated that these vendors will make less than their counterparts in ripping forums. It is unclear if this is a function of the specialized nature of this data or the likelihood of successfully manipulating this information. Regardless, this finding demonstrates that there may be distinct differences in vendor revenues based on where they advertise their products.

Though sellers have the potential to make a profit whether or not they provide usable data, buyers face much greater risks of loss as they may have no way to generate revenue if data is inactive or missing (Herley & Florencio, 2010). The prospective revenue for buyers was limited to dumps in this analysis due to the low rate of successful transactions reported for CVV and eBay/PayPal data (see Table 3.3). The findings demonstrated that buyers may make a substantive profit from the purchase of stolen data, even when purchased in small lots (see Table 3.7). Using the median direct loss from identity theft as an estimate for buyers' revenues, buyers could potentially earn a combined $470,400 from credit

Table 3.7 Estimated buyers' profits for dumps segmented by credit and bank account data by forum type

Identity 50 lot					100 lot			
Probability: 25	50	75	100	25	50	75	100	

Lot	25	50	75	100	25	50	75	100
Credit cards								
Non-ripping forums								
300	351,000.00	702,000.00	1,053,000.00	1,404,000.00	702,000.00	1,404,000.00	2,106,000.00	2,808,000.00
1148	1,964,912.63	3,929,825.25	5,894,737.88	7,859,650.50	3,929,825.25	7,859,650.50	11,789,475.75	15,719,301.00
Ripping forums								
300	82,500.00	165,000.00	247,500.00	330,000.00	165,000.00	330,000.00	495,000.00	660,000.00
1148	403,998.00	807,996.00	1,211,994.00	1,615,992.00	807,996.00	1,615,992.00	2,423,988.00	3,231,984.00
Debit cards								
Non-ripping forums								
200	204,750.00	409,500.00	614,250.00	819,000.00	409,500.00	819,000.00	1,228,500.00	1,638,000.00
551	653,050.13	1,306,100.25	1,959,150.38	2,612,200.50	1,306,100.25	2,612,200.50	3,918,300.75	5,224,401.00
Ripping forums								
200	52,500.00	105,000.00	157,500.00	210,000.00	105,000.00	210,000.00	315,000.00	420,000.00
551	134,898.00	269,796.00	404,694.00	539,592.00	269,796.00	539,592.00	809,388.00	1,079,184.00

and debit card dump purchases. Even at a 25% probability of successful transactions, buyers could earn between $351,000 and $1,964,912.63 in non-ripping forums, and $82,500 and $403,998 in ripping forums. These figures were somewhat lower when factoring in bank account losses, as buyers may make no profit at the 25% probability level with bank account information. However, buyers may have generated over $500,000 in total revenue at the 50% probability level with a lot of 50 dumps. This figure also increased substantially at the 100 dump lot level, ranging from a combined $5,748,000 at the 25% probability level to $2,689,800 at 100% probability of success.

The rate of return is also substantively higher when utilizing the average direct loss for credit or debit card data. Buyers potentially earned up to a combined amount of $7,360,643 for credit card data and $3,148,793 for bank account data at the 50 dump lot level. This figure was even greater at the 100 dump lot level, ranging from $476,760 at the 25% probability level to $6,303,585 at 100% probability for bank account data alone. Credit card revenues are even larger, reaching over $14 million dollars in the event all instances of feedback are accurate. These estimates demonstrated that data sellers received an extremely small fraction of the actual value of their products, as has been observed with the sale of stolen goods in the real world (e.g. Schneider, 2005).

Summary

This chapter clearly demonstrates that the economics of stolen data markets are affected by a range of factors associated with the practices of buyers and sellers. Our findings support the assertion by Herley and Florencio that the prices of data were a demonstration of the level of trust in sellers' products. The regression models presented on the price for data reflected the potential for multiple markets operating within this sample of forums. The conditions within a forum that demonstrated seller legitimacy and the language of the market participants were associated with higher prices. Sellers who were less legitimate were, however, associated with lower prices for most products supporting the notion that there are lemon markets operating to sell stolen data (Herley & Florencio, 2010).

There were also notable differences in the prospective profits of sellers and buyers based on the levels of trust demonstrated by positive and negative feedback provided. The results suggest that sellers were able to directly profit from any transaction, though data buyers experienced far fewer successful exchanges based on feedback than the total number of advertisements documented (e.g. Franklin et al., 2007; Herley & Florencio, 2010). Dumps, or bank and credit card data, comprised the largest proportion of products purchased though the price range for this information varied dramatically. This issue was also evident across both CVV and eBay/PayPal data despite these products having a smaller proportion of the market (see also Franklin et al., 2007; Motoyama et al., 2011). In addition, CVV and eBay data had higher price points within markets with a greater proportion of ripping complaints. This may be a function of the unique properties of this data and its potential value for unskilled actors to use to engage in fraud. Thus, the conditions of a lemon market for data may be identified by more than just low prices, but also the utility of each type of data sold.

Using the average or median price points for all forms of data demonstrate that sellers have the potential to earn hundreds of thousands of dollars from the sale of data. In fact, when the earnings from all product types are combined, sellers may have earned almost $1 million using smaller lot size estimates and over $2 million using larger lots. These figures demonstrate that selling data is a profitable venture and may account for the longevity of the markets included in this sample of forums (e.g. Holt, 2013).

Data buyers' returns had similarly high range, though it would appear that their profits could be substantially greater than those of data sellers (Herley & Florencio, 2010). Buyers have the potential to earn millions of dollars even when controlling for a low probability of useful data or successful transactions. In fact, buyer profits are easily in the hundreds of thousands even when calculating returns with smaller lots of data. There were, however, fewer successful transactions evident in the ripping forums included in this sample. This finding further reinforces the concept of lemon markets for data (Herley & Florencio, 2010). Thus, buyers appear to face substantively greater risk of loss than sellers within data markets. The tremendous return on investment may, however, explain why individuals are willing to purchase data even from unknown vendors (see Herley & Florencio, 2010). In the event that data is actually functional for use in fraud, buyers may be able to easily offset their losses and garner revenue from victims.

In light of the clear differences noted in pricing structures between ripping and non-ripping forums, there is a need to understand the relationships between all market actors and their organization within and across forums. In turn, we may be able to better identify the structural factors that drive differences between potential lemon markets and more organized forums. We will examine these issues in depth in the following chapter using qualitative analyses.

REFERENCES

Akerlov, G. A. (1970). The market for "lemons": Quality, uncertainty, and the market mechanism. *The Quarterly Journal of Economics, 84,* 488–500.

Cashell, B., Jackson, W. D., Jickling, M., & Webel, B. (2004). *The economic impact of cyber-attacks.* Congressional Research Service, Library of Congress.

Computer Security Institute. (2010). *Computer crime and security survey.* Retrieved June 3, 2011, from http://www.cybercrime.gov/FBI2010.pdf

Dhanjani, N., & Rios, B. (2008). *Bad sushi: Beating phishers at their own game.* Presented at the Annual Blackhat Meetings, Las Vegas, NV.

Franklin, J., Paxson, V., Perrig, A., & Savage, S. (2007). *An inquiry into the nature and cause of the wealth of internet miscreants.* Paper presented at CCS07, October 29–November 2, 2007, Alexandria, VA.

Harrell, E., & Langton, L. (2013). *Victims of Identity Theft, 2012.* Washington, DC: US Department of Justice, Bureau of Justice Statistics. Retrieved from http://www.bjs.gov/content/pub/pdf/vit12.pdf

Herley, C., & Florencio, D. (2010). Nobody sells gold for the price of silver: Dishonesty, uncertainty and the underground economy. In T. Moor, D. J. Pym, & C. Ioannidis (Eds.), *Economics of information security and privacy* (pp. 35–53). New York: Springer.

Holt, T. J. (2013). Exploring the social organization and structure of stolen data markets. *Global Crime, 14,* 155–174.

Holt, T. J., & Kilger, M. (2012). Know Your Enemy: The social dynamics of hacking. *The Honeynet Project.* Retrieved from https://www.honeynet.org/papers/socialdynamics

Holt, T. J., & Lampke, E. (2010). Exploring stolen data markets on-line: Products and market forces. *Criminal Justice Studies, 23,* 33–50.

Holt, T. J., & Smirnova, O. (2014). *Examining the structure, organization, and processes of the international market for stolen data.* Washington, DC: US Department of Justice. Retrieved from https://www.ncjrs.gov/pdffiles1/nij/grants/245375.pdf

Holt, T. J., Smirnova, O., & Chua, Y.-T. (2013). An exploration of the factors affecting the advertised price for stolen data. *eCrime Researchers Summit (eCRS), 2013,* pp. 1–10. IEEE.

Holt, T. J., Smirnova, O., Chua, Y.-T., & Copes, H. (2015). *Examining the risk reduction strategies of actors in online criminal markets.* Global Crime, 16(2), 81–103.

Kshetri, N. (2006). The simple economics of cybercrimes. *Security & Privacy, IEEE, 4*(1), 33–39.

McAfee. (2013). *The economic impact of cybercrime and cyber espionage July 2013.* Center for Strategic and International Studies, McAfee. Retrieved from http://www.mcafee.com/us/resources/reports/rp-economic-impact-cybercrime.pdf

McAfee. (2014). *Net losses: Estimating the global cost of cybercrime (economic impact of cybercrime II)*. Center for Strategic and International Studies, McAfee. Retrieved from http://www.mcafee.com/us/resources/reports/rp-economic-impact-cybercrime2.pdf

Moore, T., Clayton, R., & Anderson, R. (2009). The economics of online crime. *Journal of Economic Perspectives, 23*(3), 3–20.

Motoyama, M., McCoy, D., Levchenko, K., Savage, S., & Voelker, G. M. (2011). An analysis of underground forums. *IMC'11*, 71–79.

Olivier, J., & Norberg, M. N. (2010). Positively skewed data: Revisiting the box-cox power transformation. *IJPR, 3*, 68–75.

Peretti, K. K. (2009). Data breaches: What the underground world of "carding" reveals. *Santa Clara Computer and High Technology Law Journal, 25*, 375–413.

Ponemon Institute. (2014). *2014 Cost of Cyber Crime Study: United Kingdom*. Traverse City, MI: Ponemon Institute.

Schneider, J. L. (2005). Stolen-goods markets: Methods of disposal. *British Journal of Criminology, 45*, 129–140.

Seals, T. (2014). 2014 so far: The year of the data breach. *Infosecurity Magazine*, August 12. Retrieved from http://www.infosecurity-magazine.com/news/2014-the-year-of-the-data-breach/

Stone-gross, B. Abman, R., Kemmerer, R. A., Kruegel, C., Steigerwald, D. G., & Vigna, G. (2013). *The underground economy of fake antivirus software*. In Economics of Information Security and Privacy III (pp.58-78). Springer: New York.

Symantec Corporation. (2012). *Symantec Internet security threat report, Volume 17*. Retrieved from http://www.symantec.com/threatreport/

Wehinger, F. (2011). The Dark Net: Self-regulation dynamics of illegal online markets for identities and related services. *Intelligence and Security Informatics Conference*, 209–213.

Yip, M., Webber, C., & Shadbolt, N. (2013). Trust among cybercriminals? Carding forums, uncertainty, and implications for policing. *Policing and Society, 23*, 1–24.

CHAPTER 4

The Social Organization of Actors in Stolen Data Markets

Abstract This chapter discusses social organization frameworks, and applies Best and Luckenbill's framework model to the study of stolen data market participants. The framework recognizes five different types of social organizations (loners, colleagues, peers, teams, and formal organizations) based on characteristics such as mutual association, mutual participation, elaborate division of labor, and extended organization. Based on these characteristics of organizational complexity, stolen data forums operate concurrently at different levels of complexity. While some forums have longer duration of operations, others provide evidence for the sophisticated division of labor via specialized roles for members. Hence, the differentiation depends on the nature of the transaction more than on the nature of the forum.

Keywords Social organization • Colleagues • Formal organization • Trust • Escrow

As noted in the previous chapter, there are various processes within the stolen data market that suggest there may be multiple markets operating concurrently. There may be differences between participants in these markets on the basis of the complex organizational hierarchies noted that facilitate transactions, such as administrators who can establish and operate as escrow agents (Holt & Lampke, 2010; Motoyama, McCoy, Levchenko, Savage, & Voelker, 2011; Wehinger, 2011). At the same time, there also appears to be a tiered structure of participants, whether buyers or sellers, which creates multiple organizational dynamics that vary based on the forum (Herley & Florencio, 2010; Wehinger, 2011). In order to explore these issues, this chapter will explore the ways in which actors involved in the sale of stolen data organically organize and explore any variations in the practices across forums generally. We will first consider the structure of this framework, then describe the analysis techniques applied, and examine the organizational practices in depth.

Social Organization Frameworks

To examine the organizational dynamics of stolen data markets, we utilize a sociological model of social organization since they provide valuable frameworks to measure relationships between deviants, and how such relationships function on- or off-line (Adler & Adler, 2006; Best & Luckenbill, 1994; Decker, Bynum, & Weisel, 1998; Holt, 2009; Mann & Sutton, 1998; Meyer, 1989). One of the most comprehensive and well-applied social organization frameworks was developed by Best and Luckenbill (1994) to identify associations between individuals and groups, and the transactions they engage in. This framework can also be used to understand the way that social relationships affect individual positions within a clique or network. At the same time, this framework considers the role or pattern of action individuals play in larger social networks and subcultures (Best & Luckenbill, 1994). In turn, social organization frameworks can be used to explore the presence or absence of collegial associations between actors, coordinated or purposive roles between participants, managerial positions, and their duration over time.

The Best and Luckenbill (1994) framework of social organization views deviant behavior as a transaction, where behavior is focused toward a particular goal. In deviant transactions, participants are oriented toward behaviors that bring them a degree of gratification whether economic or otherwise. Any transaction has a division of labor that can vary from an individual act to a multi-person scheme with distinct roles for each participant. For instance, prostitution typically involves a sex worker and their client (e.g. Holzman & Pines, 1982; Scott & Dedel, 2006), while a drug trafficking network incorporates multiple high-level actors working in conjunction with low-level street dealers who distribute product (Adler & Adler, 2006; Cross, 2000; Decker & Chapman, 2008; Jacobs, 1996). Finally, transactions have "flexible coordination," in that individuals can adapt their behavior to meet the needs of a particular situation or disruption technique designed to affect deviant behavior (Best & Luckenbill, 1994, p. 75).

There are three forms of transactions in this framework: individual deviance, deviant exchanges, and deviant exploitation. Individual deviance requires a single participant for an act to be completed. For instance, individuals who engage in cutting and self-harm may discuss their activities with others online, but need not have any help to engage in deviance (Adler & Adler, 2006). Deviant exchanges require two or more actors working in collaborative but distinct roles to achieve an end (Best & Luckenbill, 1994). These individuals may be weakly tied and interested only in an immediate exchange (as in the case of prostitution), or more strongly tied and seeking long-term relationships (as in drug distribution networks). Deviant exploitation, however, requires two actors who work in conflicting roles such that one is an offender and the other is a target or victim of the offender (Best & Luckenbill, 1994, p. 75).

Best and Luckenbill argue that deviants organize in different ways based on the form of deviant transactions they engage in over time. The structure of social relationships vary based on four elements of organizational complexity: (1) mutual associations assess the presence of relationships between individuals, (2) mutual participation considers whether individuals participate in deviance as a collective or alone, (3) elaborate division of labor explores the structure and coordination of roles between deviants, and (4) extended organization assesses how long deviant activities extend over time across virtual and/or real spaces (Best & Luckenbill, 1994) These characteristics create a continuum of organizational sophistication with five forms of deviant organizations: loners, colleagues, peers, teams, and formal organizations (see Table 4.1).

Loners constitute the least sophisticated form of organization as they do not associate with other deviants frequently and offend alone. Colleagues are the next most sophisticated since they interact with other deviants to form a subculture based on shared knowledge and offending techniques. Though subcultural associations engender the formation of networks, colleagues neither offend together nor have any division of labor. Peers, however, have all the characteristics of colleagues and engage in deviance or crime with others. They do not have any specialized roles in offending nor do they persist over time. Teams are more sophisticated in that they offend together for some period of time and have an elaborate division of labor used when engaging in deviance. The most sophisticated deviant organizations are formal organization, encompassing all aspects of teams in addition to an extended duration across time and space (Best & Luckenbill, 1994).

Table 4.1 Best and Luckenbill's (1994) social organization framework

Form of organization	Characteristics			
	Mutual association	Mutual participation	Elaborate division of labor	Extended organization
Loners	No	No	No	No
Colleagues	Yes	No	No	No
Peers	Yes	Yes	No	No
Teams	Yes	Yes	Yes	No
Formal organizations	Yes	Yes	Yes	Yes

From Best and Luckenbill (1994), p. 12

The Best and Luckenbill (1994) framework is beneficial for researchers as it provides a high degree of flexibility in the identification of organizational structures involved in any form of deviance. In fact, multiple forms of organization may operate concurrently or vary over time and across locations. Furthermore, this model accounts not only for traditional hierarchical forms of organization, but also for network models that are driven by normative relationships between participants based on exchanges or transactions (Best & Luckenbill, 1994). Thus, this framework is ideal to explore the associations between actors in on-line markets which could vary from site to site, product to product, and over time.

Examining Social Organization in Stolen Data Markets

Though researchers have explored the social dynamics of the market for stolen data, few have considered how the market operates from an organizational standpoint (see Holt, 2013). As identified in Chap. 2, it is clear that stolen data sales and services are a form of deviant exchange based on the movement of data from a seller to buyers, or from buyers to service providers in the context of cash-out services and drops providers (Franklin, Paxson, Perrig, & Savage, 2007; Herley & Florencio, 2010; Holt, 2013; Holt & Lampke, 2010; Motoyama et al., 2011; Wehinger, 2011).

To explore the ways that actors within the market for stolen data are organized, we used grounded theory analysis techniques (Bryant & Charmaz, 2010; Charmaz, 2006; Corbin & Strauss, 1990; 2007) to develop the data, while concurrently applying guiding questions from Best and Luckenbill (1994) and other qualitative researchers who have applied this framework. We also focus the unit of analysis at both the individual and forum levels to understand the actor and the environment interaction to influence transactions and their organization (Best & Luckenbill, 1994). At the individual level, we considered the ways that "deviant actors organize themselves to pursue their deviant activities" and how "these basic forms differ in organizational features, such as division of labor, coordination among the deviant actors, and objectives" (Best & Luckenbill, 1994, p. 12).

At the forum level, we consider multiple questions to address how individuals and the environment are organized over time. Since the forum data extends over a period of years across many of the forums, we considered the ways that organizational patterns change over time by asking "what conditions shape the development and transformation of organizational forms," and "how do organizational forms change over time, and what conditions account for these changes?" (Best & Luckenbill, 1994, p. 12). The findings should not be considered as conclusive evidence of behavioral and organizational change, though the substantial sample of forums over time provided a basis of comparison to identify prospective changes across all sites or isolated patterns within a single forum (see also Holt, 2009, 2013).

These concepts were used to structure the analyses, along with questions utilized in prior studies of the social organization of gang activity (Decker et al., 1998) and computer hackers (Holt, 2009; Meyer, 1989). These studies provide valuable operationalizations of concepts to understand the social organization practices of offenders using three sets of questions. First, we considered the complexity of division of labor, on the basis of evidence of co-offending and any evidence of a segmented chain of activity in the performance of an offense. Additionally, we consider the presence of unique groups, direct or indirect evidence of membership, and stratification of roles or specialization (see also Decker et al., 1998). Second, we assessed the coordination of roles on the basis of codified rules or regulations on relationships, and evidence of how those rules are enforced (Decker et al., 1998). Finally, we considered purposive relationships between groups through any evidence of co-offending between groups and/or leisure activities that could be observed (Decker et al., 1998).

These questions were used to refine the concepts identified during the open phase of grounded theory analyses (see Chap. 4 for details on grounded theory analyses; Bryant & Charmaz, 2010; Charmaz, 2006; Corbin & Strauss, 1990, 2007). The inductively generated findings were then compared against the Best and Luckenbill (1994) framework to consider the social organization of buyers, sellers, moderators, and participants in these forums. Each of the four components of this model, mutual association, mutual participation, division of labor, and extended duration, will be discussed in detail using respondents' comments or observations where appropriate.

Assessing Mutual Association and Participation in the Forums

As elaborated in Chaps. 2 and 3, there appear to be multiple markets operating concurrently within this sample of forums. The presence of rippers, differential pricing structures, and product distributions across forums demonstrate that there are markets with greater general legitimacy which may increase the likelihood of success in any transaction. Regardless, the forums are structured to facilitate deviant transactions between interested individuals based on the sale of data or services to others. The buyer and seller comprise the two parties involved in any transaction, though in some instances money launderers and encashment services operate through partnerships and operate in small groups. Though data sellers need only engage with the buyer to exchange data for currency, encashers cannot obtain funds without data. For example, a seller in Forum 13 advertised their services to place funds onto ATM cards that could then be used to obtain money from stolen accounts. The ad specifically uses the term "we" in the text, suggesting that they may have collaborators assisting them. Additionally, the seller clearly indicates that a degree of cooperation was needed with the buyer in order to complete a transaction:

> Provision of services for the identification of electronic payment systems and preparation of ATM cards for drops [RU].
>
> **WM [WebMoney] registration process:**
> We provide you with a photocopy of the passport. Using this information you register a new WMID [WebMoney Identification Number]. You receive a formal certificate under the data of the photocopied passport, you pay for the application to receive a personal certificate. You give us the data of the newly registered WMID used during registration. We write this data into the application and send them to the Certification Center. After a while you receive the personal certification for this WMID.
> ONLY you will have access to this WMID, and no one else.

Terms of service:

- We have the right to refuse to work after accepting payment in case of force majeure circumstances. If we refuse, we will return the money which we have received within a 2-day time period, after advising of the refusal. Take into account that we mean 2 BUSINESS days.
- You must understand that... the card is not yours, it belongs to another person and at any moment he [the victim] can block it. Our task is not to allow this, and up to now we have done this well.
- Our service is not liable if your account is closed by the payment system for fraud and various fraudulent actions.

Such ads demonstrate that there is a degree of specialized knowledge among participants within these forums. Their mutual participation in offending appears limited, and based largely around the completion of a given transaction. Thus, actors within these forums appear to be operating more as colleagues or peers to facilitate short-term exchanges or transactions over time (see Herley & Florencio, 2010; Holt & Lampke, 2010).

In much the same way, the use of feedback in the forums constitutes its own form of a social transaction. The process of completing a transaction outside of the forum requires both parties to accept some degree of risk. In order to minimize the level of risk others may experience, buyers can post their experience and describe how the seller operates. Such comments are not mandated by the forums, but are useful to promote trust between participants. Positive feedback can establish an individual's reputation, and demonstrate that a buyer is an active participant in the larger community (Holt & Lampke, 2010; Motoyama et al., 2011; Wehinger, 2011). For instance, an individual in Forum 1 sold credit cards from around the world. He received a number of positive comments from buyers as evident in these posts: "everything went well. You can trust this person"; "I got 2 car[d]s. Everything okay! My trust!"; and "the carton [card] is in good working order! I bought it and I will only buy from him in the future. There were no problems. Thanks!" Similarly, an individual offered his services as a money launderer and encasher, and received multiple positive responses from customers:

Killz: I withdrew cash everything was okay
Cypher: Everything was excellent and online.
Iglio: I worked with this person everything was ok

> **Horvath:** I laundered wm without any problems. Everything was good.
> **Nash:** This is not the first time that I have worked with the TS, everything was tiptop!
> **Nod31:** I use the services... twice and everything was precise and the payment was on time according to the contract. service +1

This sort of feedback demonstrates that the sellers are reliable, particularly when repeat clients describe their experience (Holt & Lampke, 2010). In turn, the participants in the thread are spending their own social capital to affect the reputation of the seller.

In the event that a seller distributes inactive or invalid data, or takes payments without delivering product, they can expect buyers will post negative feedback about their experience (Holt & Lampke, 2010). Public comments of this sort are a transaction that trades on the buyers' reputation to cause harm to the seller. Recognition of a bad sale highlights who prospective buyers should avoid in order to minimize their risk of loss. This was evident in a series of posts from Forum 4. A seller named Jackson posted an advertisement for credit card data from various countries and received substantial negative feedback based on his use of bad data and poor response times. Prospective and actual customers noted this in their posts, stating:

> **Nickly:** registration [on the sellers personal shop website is] temporary disable[d] so what is the essence or advantage of this advert here when someone cannot make reg[istration]
> **Stan:** They have been selling the same dump since April, very stale, support is no help!
> **Nickly:** yes Stan bulshit [SIC] garbage dumps in his shop...all claims dumps there are dead since April and is still claiming 90 percent valid... lol buyer be careful
> **Vendor:** dumps extremely low working % You will be lucky to card yourself a happy meal with one of these shit ass dumps... Thumbs down.

This feedback demonstrates what constitutes an untrustworthy vendor who poses a risk to the larger market of buyers and sellers. In turn, such vendors may experience lower sales relative to actors with more positive reviews (see Holt & Lampke, 2010; Motoyama et al., 2011).

There are risks for individuals who choose to participate in the public advertising process by posting positive or negative feedback. Since reviews are not mandatory, a seller or other forum users may challenge a post with negative feedback. For instance, sellers may point out when a negative experience stems from user error in order minimize any fallout they may experience from poor reviews (Holt & Lampke, 2010). This was demonstrated in Forum 5 when a customer named DILS bought dedicated server space from a seller. DILS posted a negative comment stating: "it's not worth getting a dedicated [server] from him. 2 times I got one from him and even for a week they didn't work he shuts off accounts specially." The seller then posted a relatively detailed response to this negative feedback, including content from their chat logs outside of the forum to demonstrate what actually happened:

> Prof: Dear smarty DILS! Let's dot all the i's so that everyone understands what's going on. First of all, I only sold one dedicated to you. and second (according to your own words) .your friend supposedly for your friends supposedly for you, here is an excerpt from the correspondence:
> "DILS: it simply already the second thing that happened
> Prof: we mean the second time? in this asya [instance] I have no such events in the history
> DILS: I tossed beans [money] over to webmoney my account is r298…but we came to an agreement my friend…"
> I'm not telepathic and can't see who is giving dedicateds to whom or who is reselling them and even more so I can't bear any liability for this.
> Furthermore - if in your words the ded[icated server] did not work for a week already - this is not in any way associated with me disconnecting accounts, as you said yourself, already you can't call your story anything more than bullshit nonsense.
> Well and that's the main portion of our communication with you:
> DILS: Hi!\
> Prof: hey
> DILS: I have a question for you. I bought a ded[icated server] from you
> Prof: well
> DILS: it hasn't been working for weeks now what should I do I haven't been able to do anything [with] it
> Prof: if a week already – then I think nothing
> DILS: [not] even download maybe you can give another deed? because I just can't use it
> Prof: well alas, the guarantee is only 5 days, and what you did there or didn't do there I have no way of checking is that logical?
> DILS: ok tks [thanks]
>
> Thanks and I went off to go scribble some backbiting lines. I'm freaking out over you. really :)

This example highlights that sellers can engage buyers in their threads so as to ensure that they are not mischaracterized, or their reputations unfairly affected (Holt & Lampke, 2010). As a result, the review process appears to be a peer-driven process while many of the financial transactions that take place outside of the forum may be simple one-to-one exchanges. Stolen data markets may, as a result, operate in a similar fashion to illicit on-line markets for prostitution where customers discuss and rate the services of sex workers (Holt & Blevins, 2007; Milrod & Weitzer, 2012; Sharp & Earle, 2003), or even more legitimate markets such as eBay or Amazon (Aspers, 2011).

Division of Labor Between Market Actors

It is clear that the market promotes associations between individuals, and promotes a specific set of subcultural norms for seller and buyer activity. At the same time, the distribution of products advertised demonstrates that there is some degree of specialization among sellers. Individuals could purchase virtually any service demonstrating that the market for stolen data enables fraud and cybercrime from data acquisition to data manipulation (Franklin et al., 2007; Holt & Lampke, 2010; Motoyama et al., 2011; Wehinger, 2011). There was, however, little information to discern whether advertisements that use the term "we" when describing their services were actually supported by an organized group of offenders. Such information was largely absent from any advertisements with one exception: drops services. Individuals who could either accept goods or forward money were part of larger networks, where there was a division of labor between the person who purchased a product, received it, and then dealt with the item. This was noted in an ad from Forum 4 where the seller indicated how their service worked, including what products they would work with and the percentage of funds that could be made by the drops user:

Drops for stuff in US 30-45%
We give a stuff drops in US.
All services drop tested 3.2 test parcels [packages]. They signed a contract and pay the salaries (net cash), which significantly reduces kidki [dead or unsent] drops and increases the life of loot, we loot work from a month or more until they get bored. Quality of divorce [separation from recipient to sender] drops at a high level to see this, who works with us the first month or year.

Conditions:
- 30–45% on - International Dispatch, working only on this scheme

- 50/50 stuff (do, for example, 2 identical cameras-one refer to you).
Goods that we accept and % payment is done as an example and a list is not complete, the entire list is in the admin panel. List is updated frequently and increasing.

Notebook:
Sony Vaio - P, Z, TT, AW, SR, CS, NS, FW - 40%
MacBook - 40-45%
Asus - 35%

Cameras:
Canon and Nikon - 40%
lenses to them - 40%
Mobile phones - 35%
- The main advantages of our service - you take the drops, the amount that you need and make a number of products that you see fit, in that there are no restrictions. All data that you make to the panel on the new premise, the drop gets in their panel information by email and sms, which greatly reduces the possibility of a drop pass your product.

Since goods must be purchased, received, and subsequently dealt with, these schemes required a degree of separation and coordination between participants. Since networks of drops may dissipate quickly and do not require much by way of specialized knowledge, they may constitute peers or teams depending on their structure (Best & Luckenbill, 1994).

Aside from drops providers, there appeared to be a natural segmentation between data sellers and manipulation service providers. There was no evidence in any of the forums sampled to suggest that dumps vendors also advertised web hosting or cash-out services, nor did drops services offer dumps or CVV data. Individual vendors also appeared to have no specific connections, recommendations, or negotiated price breaks with other service providers. Vendors simply offered their wares or services with no working relationships to other market actors. As a result, the collegial relationships enabled by the forums do not facilitate the formation of specialized groups of offenders working in concert to commit data breaches and manipulation. Actors appear to be interested in their own profit margins and do not publicly promote services to buyers as this may influence their position within the market (Herley & Florencio, 2010; Wehinger, 2011).

Though sellers would not promote the services of their colleagues or competitors, they noted when their products were advertised on multiple forums in an attempt to demonstrate their reputation and reliability. For instance, an individual in Forum 2 sold log files obtained from compromised computers, which contained sensitive personal information, usernames, and password data. The seller indicated that their products were advertised on three additional forums and provided external links to that content, with a note stating that their product: "passed testing [by forum administrators] on [link removed]." This information is a key way for the seller to demonstrate the legitimacy of their products and attract buyers who could check these other sites. Advertisements with cross-listed external links were found in seven of the legitimate forums, and were largely absent from the ripping forums in this sample. Such information demonstrates there are some purposive relationships between forums, though they are driven entirely by sellers or buyers. Additionally, this information should not be interpreted as proof of collaborative efforts or offending by forum actors, but rather supports some vendors' concurrent participation in multiple markets.

While there is some evidence of role specialization between sellers, the enforcement of rules and regulations regarding user behaviors, whether of seller or buyer, fell to forum moderators or administrators (Chu, Holt, & Ahn, 2010; Holt & Lampke, 2010; Motoyama et al., 2011). An administrator was found in all of the forums included in this sample, though they were not typically frequent posters or heavily engaged in each thread. This is likely a result of the fact that moderators typically manage encounters between users when necessary, but do not police and micromanage all threads (e.g. Holt, 2007; Mann & Sutton, 1998).

Moderators served very specific roles in the forums, mostly focused on regulating seller activity and promoting trust between actors. For example, administrators in eight of the forums were available to test and review products offered by vendors. Product testing was an essential way for buyers to assess the reputation of a given seller, though it was not a requirement in order to post an ad. This was exemplified in the rules regarding checking from Forum 7:

> **Checking Rules**
> Checking your goods will take place voluntarily or if the administration of the forum requires it.
> Checking of goods is done by **ICQ [number removed]**
> The check last from one to three days.
> After the check, the moderator guarantees that there will not be any stupid flames in the topic and that the quality of the goods will not be discussed. The moderator will write a review on this and close the topic. If a requirement to

provide your product for testing is refused, you risk being banned, and your announcement will be erased. No money is taken for testing.
You provide the product for the test in the same configuration in which you sell it

As noted, checking products helps sellers and buyers because a positive review denotes the person they are dealing with is trustworthy (Holt & Lampke, 2010). It also adds a layer of organizational complexity to the general sales process: sellers must engage administrators in order to acquire a review. This adds to the division of specialized labor within the market, making moderators pertinent players in the organizational complexity of data markets (see Herley & Florencio, 2010; Wehinger, 2011).

Since testing or checking is optional in some forums, a seller whose products have been tested in one market may choose not to go through this process in other forums. The time needed to complete a check or obtain a written review may be viewed as unnecessary by a seller. Alternatively, if they are selling products across multiple markets, having a product checked by the most regarded forum they participate in may be more appealing. To that end, a number of sellers in this sample indicated when their products had been tested on a separate site as in this post from Forum 5:

> I would like to offer you the services for filling up your mailbox with pinodosy [spam to people from NATO countries, esp. The USA]... I HAVE UNDERGONE A CHECK ON THE CLOSED FORUM [name removed] I am also ready to undergo a check on your platform. I work both through the guarantor of any forum as well as through protection.

Similarly, a seller in Forum 4 placed the following comment at the end of his ad: "Checks have been undergone with the guarantors of the forum [name removed], and [forum name removed]." An interested buyer can seek out the reviews in order to determine a seller's prospective reputation and trustworthiness. In turn, the buyer does not have to exert any additional effort or waste data or service time with additional tests.

Since product testing was largely voluntary, sellers could weigh the decision to obtain a test relative to their potential for engagement with buyers to obtain positive reviews. This was exemplified in Forum 10 where actors lodged complaints against a seller who posted an ad for a scheme to infect users with malware in order to make money. Though the seller had their product very quickly checked by the forum moderator and a positive review posted, potential buyers complained about the seller's scheme and product. The following exchange reveals the thought process of buyers and sellers in this context:

> Goldburg: The check doesn't mean anything. The majority of cases they check theoretically (or for the presence of such), and at the same time neither in the post of the TS [Thread Starter] nor in the post of the checker is their word said about the labor input, needed [SIC] for certain skills, knowledge etc.
> TS, it would be easier to describe into words in the topic and not waste your time or anyone else's.
> TS:I can undergo a check on any board, but I don't see any sense in this because I'm selling to 10 people, two are thinking about it, another three will buy within the next few days, so whoever is interested, they will buy it, and I don't want to bother with tests on other boards and waste time on that.

In this instance, buyers felt that the test details were insufficient and that the buyer may not be a trustworthy actor. The fact that the TS was able to acquire a test indicates that they are trying to promote their product in the most efficient way possible. Such a test is not, however, mandated, making any seller question whether the effort is worth the prospective increase in buyers (Herley & Florencio, 2010; Holt & Lampke, 2010).

Three of the forums in this sample offered an alternative to testing or checking services, wherein a seller could be "verified," or vetted by the site administrators. For instance, in Forum 9, a seller could become a verified vendor by contacting the forum administrators. The process was explained in the following post:

> Support VPro Celler provides access to sellers account only after:
>
> 1. Verification via PM [Private Message] to one of forums
> 2. Talking with contacts listed inside promotional theme [advertisement] of service/vendor...

A similar comment was noted in Forum 8, where the supermoderator posted:

> **Attention!** All the Members here are advised not to deal or buy anything from Unverified Sellers! If you do so and you get scammed! We are not responsible! Only buy from those sellers who are verified! For all the Sellers who want to get themselves verified contact me through pm! :-P

Becoming a verified seller helps to demonstrate that a vendor is competent and trustworthy based on their market performance and customer feedback (Holt & Lampke, 2010; Motoyama et al., 2011). The verification process is not, however, as stringent as that of product testing, making it difficult for buyers to ensure they will have a successful transaction with a given vendor. For instance, two of the forums with verification options had a high proportion of ripping and buyer complaints. The administrator in Forum 1 indicated that their verification process was largely ineffectual as sellers were unwilling to work with him. He expressed his frustration with both buyers and sellers in the following post:

> I protect everyone from any unverified seller and write about it. It says many that these guyz don't want to pay some fee like $50 (may be they have no any money.^))) LOL and also don't want to give me their stuff 4 checking))) IT SAYS MANY! Also you can find these rippers/sellers on other forums with fake comments. THERE WILL NOT BE RIPPERS!!! AS SOON AS ANY WANTS TO BE VERIFIED THERE WILL BE CATEGORY WITH VERIFIED SELLERS (also verified seller can rip you off with good amount) you can use escrow. Also I've all stuf [SIC] whats market can provide anyone (dumps, cc, skimmers, drops) … but I don't sell anything and don't provide any service. I'm only admin and provide you with forum 4 deals and talks.

This example illustrates that verification processes are not always an effective mechanism to establish trust. Furthermore, those who are verified may still post a threat, thus sellers should carefully leverage any and all mechanisms at their disposal to ensure they are satisfied. Though verification adds a layer of interaction and complexity, it is insufficient in reducing the likelihood of ripping (Herley & Florencio, 2010). Those forums whose members are unwilling to have their products either tested or verified may be less insulated from outsiders attempting to cheat buyers (Herley & Florencio, 2010; Wehinger, 2011).

A proportion of the forum administrators in this sample also specified and operated as escrow agents or guarantors for the larger forum (see Chap. 2 for further detail). The addition of a third party as a guarantor adds a layer of organizational complexity to any transaction, though it increases the likelihood of success for all involved. Guarantors must ensure that any payment provided to a seller is withheld until such time as the buyer is satisfied with the transaction as a whole or return the funds to the buyer if necessary (Herley & Florencio, 2010; Holt & Lampke, 2010; Wehinger, 2011). This decreases the efficiency of the sales process due to the need for contact between all parties to ensure smooth delivery of products and payments. In addition, two of the sites indicated that guarantors could charge a fee for their services based on the amount being paid in the transaction. This was exemplified in a post explaining guarantor services in Forum 4:

> Guarantor services
> The guarantor of a forum has been created so that you will not be deceived... By conducting a transaction through a guarantor, you can be sure that you will not be deceived.
> Terms for working through a guarantor:
>
> 1. The buyer and the seller must reach agreement on working through a Guarantor.
> 2. The buyer and the seller must contact the Guarantor using icq.
> 3. One of the Parties to the transaction gives money to the Guarantor, and the other goods.
> 4. The guarantor's services are free up to $30. [After this amount, the guarantor will take a variable percentage of the total for their efforts. The rates are described below]
>
> up to 500 wmz - 8%
> from 500 wmz - 6%
> from 3000 wmz - 5%

The use of guarantors or escrow agents directly increases the transaction costs for buyers, and demonstrates the organizational complexity of the market for stolen data (Herley & Florencio, 2010; Wehinger, 2011). Those groups with greater capacity to regulate user posts and receive a portion of all escrow payments processed are more likely to constitute a team-driven operation rather than a more short-term organization.

In addition to managing seller reputations, administrators played a pivotal role in the management of user behavior and enforcement of codified forum rules. Each forum had its own terms for sales, and for the ways that buyers could review and post comments about any specific seller's practices. Buyers are given the ability to provide feedback, since it is the key social mechanism to warn users about rippers and informally sanction disreputable sellers. Labeling a seller as a ripper can, however, disrupt the stability of a thread and foster arguments between participants (Chu et al., 2010; Franklin et al., 2007). Such complaints may be leveraged by legitimate buyers, or by competitors or troublemakers seeking to harm the economic viability of a vendor. When negative conversations begin, this has the potential to negatively impact both the seller and the perceived legitimacy of the forum (Franklin et al., 2007).

Administrators in four of the forums established rules to minimize false claims and penalize individuals who may be posting to disrupt a seller's business. For instance, moderators from Forum 3 stated that claims of cheating or bad reviews were "Strictly Forbidden," and must be accompanied by proof of their interaction with the seller such as chat logs and proof of payment. Should these rules be violated, there were clear punishments that could be imposed, as explained in the following post:

2. Strictly forbidden.

2.1 Posting topics / messages in someone else's name. Even if it is specified that you were asked to do this.

2.1.1 To offer your goods / services in someone else's sales topic.

2.1.2 To offer goods that do not belong to you. To work as an intermediary in transactions.

2.2 To leave duplicate reviews (use editing of the previous comment).

2.2.1 To leave fictitious reviews in topics. The fact that a transaction has been carried out must be confirmed by the appropriate proof upon the first request of the administration. If this clause is violated, the user leaving a fictitious review will be banned, and perhaps even permanently.

2.3 To leave the following type of message: "TS is a burner, you shouldn't have anything to do with him." We will immediately post the blogs proving guilt.

3. Additionally.

3.1 Reviews from users with 1-10 messages who have not been on the forum for long will be deleted at the discretion of the moderator.

3.2 Only messages with reviews are to be left in the topics. All questions are to be given to the author using icq / PM.

3.3 "UP" topics are permitted only once in 4 days (96 hours). All messages from the author except the first one shall be considered to be "ups." For each new "up," deletes the previous one.

3.4 If there is a refusal to work through the forum's <u>guarantors</u> the topic will be transferred to the section <u>Suspicious Characters</u>, and the seller will be banned, perhaps even permanently.

The level of detail required for a buyer to demonstrate that they have been cheated suggests that this forum is both well organized and policed by the administrator. Furthermore, specifying the rules for both buyers and sellers and how certain actions can lead an individual to be banned or blocked from the forum is an important power to manage forum relationships. For instance, banning someone because they will not work with a guarantor is an important metric for the seller's trust and quality of products. Similarly, someone with less than ten posts may be a new participant in the market, though it is also likely that it may be a fictitious account created so as to post false claims or disrupt the market (Franklin et al., 2007). Thus, forum moderators who are interested in maintaining order may sanction and edit user content to reduce unsubstantiated claims and keep their forum free of discord.

The use of banning and/or deletion is a critical demonstration of the division of labor within a forum. Evidence of both banning and edits of posts were present across all of the forums in this sample, though there was some variation in the details. Some threads had posts with notes indicating that an administrative edit and deletion had occurred, while others simply listed the word banned next to a username in a thread though their posts remained. There were no explanations provided as to why an individual may have been banned; the moderator may have simply felt it necessary or the individual user did something inappropriate in a different thread. Regardless, the power to ban users is a critical mechanism for administrators to regulate encounters and enforce rules within forums.

Extended Duration of the Markets

Thus far, our analyses indicate that there are multiple levels of sophistication operating concurrently within the market for stolen data. The individual buyers and sellers appear less organized relative to the forum operators due to their influence on the market transactions and the ways buyers and sellers can engage one another. With that in mind, we will consider the final element of organizational sophistication within the Best and Luckenbill (1994) framework: extended duration. In the context of forums, duration is affected in part by the creation date of the website which is facilitated by site operators. At the same time, participants who engage in site over a long period of time would suggest they are stable and persistent players within the market. Thus, the extended duration of a group over time appears to affect all players in the market for stolen data.

There are two key data points that can be used to assess the temporal duration of actors within the forums. The first source is the date of the first and last post of the threads from each forum in the sample (see Table 4.2), establishing the range of time the forum has had active participants. Three of the forums in this sample had posts dating back to 2007, meaning the forum has had active participants engaged in transactions over a several year period. The oldest advertisement in this sample was first posted in Forum 13 on June 6, 2007. The seller offered passport scans and identity documents made to order using stolen personal information acquired from various sources. Both the ad and the seller were still active and operating at the time of data collection, though this may be an outlier as the majority of ads in this sample were posted within the last two years (see Table 4.2).

Four of the forums in this sample also operated over two or more years, suggesting they are established markets. The remaining forums in the sample included less than three months to more than seven months of posts. Such a range is in keeping with prior research on the hacker community using on-line data (e.g. Holt, 2007; Holt, Strumsky, Smirnova, & Kilger, 2012; Meyer, 1989).

The second pertinent measure to assess the duration of a group over time is the date an individual joined a particular forum. Many on-line communities provide the date when a user registered with the site, or made their first post in order to identify how long they have actively participated in

Table 4.2 Duration of forum participation by join date of user and post dates[a]

Forum number	First join date	Last join date	First post date	Last post date	Number of months
1	1/1/2011	8/1/2011	12/31/2010	7/21/2011	7.2
2	NA	NA	12/1/2010	2/23/2011	2.73
4	8/31/2009	2/28/2011	10/3/2009	12/25/2011	26.73
5	11/10/2005	12/11/2010	6/6/2008	12/11/2010	30.17
6	12/15/2009	8/2/2011	2/5/2009	11/14/2011	33.3
7	12/1/2010	12/20/2011	12/26/2010	7/9/2011	6.43
8	8/1/2008	12/1/2011	4/1/2009	11/1/2011	31
9	4/1/2011	7/1/2011	4/1/2011	7/21/2011	3.67
10	4/13/2009	3/8/2011	4/10/2010	3/7/2011	10.9
11	2/23/2007	2/25/2012	5/9/2007	2/25/2012	57.53
12	5/1/2007	6/10/2011	11/7/2007	11/9/2011	60.07
13	12/18/2004	8/1/2011	6/6/2007	7/25/2011	61.63

[a]Forum 3 excluded from this analysis due to limited data

discussions. This information more accurately captures how long a forum has been active, as the date of a user's first post may be well before the first post captured in this sample of threads.

The date of users' first posts was available for all but two of the forums in this sample, and demonstrates that four of the forums have been operational for years, going back to 2004 (Forum 13), 2005 (Forum 5), and 2007, respectively (Forums 11 and 12). Four additional forums had members join in 2008 and 2009, suggesting that the sites have been active for much longer periods of time than what is captured in the sample of threads. The remaining forums had members join more recently, suggesting they may be less established than the others in this sample.

In all, more than half of the forums sampled (61.5 %) appear to constitute formal organizations based on their extended duration over time. It is important to note that Forum 8 was one of the two designated ripping forums in this sample, yet had members posting since 2008, and had over two years of posts in this sample of threads. Despite its temporal persistence, the forum had limited managerial oversight suggesting it may not comprise a formal organization as per Best and Luckenbill (1994). The remaining forums in this sample may either be in early operational phases or reflect the generally short lifespan of forums in the underground (Holt, 2009; Holt & Lampke, 2010; Meyer, 1989).

Summary

In general, this chapter demonstrates that these stolen data forums operate at various levels of sophistication concurrently. Sellers and buyers operate as colleagues, and in some cases peers, to facilitate successful transactions and engage in exchange of data outside of the forums. The collegial environment of these forums enables individuals to gain access to various partnerships to achieve a specific goal (Franklin et al., 2007; Holt & Lampke, 2010; Motoyama et al., 2011). An individual could buy cards from one seller, and then pay an encasher or launderer who can move funds from those accounts. Though sellers may want to develop long-term relationships, buyers can engage anyone based on the availability of products and access to resources. In this way, the market engenders a division of labor between participants based on their ability to offer certain products and services (Franklin et al., 2007; Herley & Florencio, 2010; Holt & Lampke, 2010; Motoyama et al., 2011; Wehinger, 2011).

The public nature of posting and reviews are peer-driven, since actors can engage one another and influence action through their recommendations. Sellers who receive positive feedback may be more likely to gain multiple clients over time, while negative feedback may lead to sanctions from administrators (Holt & Lampke, 2010; Motoyama et al., 2011). Forum administrators can ban users on the basis of fraudulent claims in order to moderate user activity. At the same time, they can offer assistance to sellers through testing and review of products. The use of various mechanisms to identify quality sellers helps to minimize the risk of loss for market actors, though the lack of consistency with which banning or product testing services were available suggests that there are low barriers to enter the market (Herley & Florencio, 2010; Holt & Lampke, 2010; Motoyama et al., 2011). Unscrupulous venders may be able to penetrate a well-regulated market, or operate freely within deregulated forums, leaving buyers to determine the reliability of a seller.

This chapter also demonstrates that these forums vary in their persistence over time and presence of purposive relationships between groups. Eight of the forums sampled constitute formal organizations on the basis of their duration over time, while the others in this data set appear to be driven by teams due to their short duration and generally limited organizational complexity. One of the forums with an extended duration was also a ripping forum, suggesting that any market may be able to operate for a long period of time regardless of its reputation (Herley & Florencio, 2010; Wehinger, 2011). Thus, there is a need for deeper exploration into the network structure of market actors to understand any differences in the relationships observed between buyers and sellers in ripping and non-ripping forums alike.

REFERENCES

Adler, P. A., & Adler, P. (2006). Self-injurers as loners: The social organization of solitary deviance. *Deviant Behavior, 26*, 345–378.

Aspers, P. (2011). *Markets*. Cambridge: Polity Press.

Best, J., & Luckenbill, D. F. (1994). *Organizing deviance* (2nd ed.). New Jersey: Prentice Hall.

Bryant, A., & Charmaz, K. (2010). *The Sage handbook of grounded theory*. Thousand Oaks, CA: Sage.

Charmaz, K. (2006). *Constructing grounded theory: A practical guide through qualitative analysis*. Thousand Oaks, CA: Sage.

Chu, B., Holt, T. J., & Ahn, G. J. (2010). *Examining the creation, distribution, and function of malware on-line.* Technical Report for National Institute of Justice. NIJ Grant No. 2007-IJ-CX-0018. Retrieved from http://www.ncjrs.gov/pdffiles1/nij/grants/230112.pdf

Corbin, J., & Strauss, A. (1990). Grounded theory research: Procedures, canons, and evaluative criteria. *Qualitative Sociology, 13,* 3–2.

Corbin, J., & Strauss, A. (2007). *Basics of doing qualitative research: Techniques and procedures for developing grounded theory.* Thousand Oaks, CA: Sage.

Cross, J. C. (2000). Passing the buck: Risk avoidance and risk management in the illegal/informal drug trade. *International Journal of Sociology and Social Policy, 20,* 68–94.

Decker, S. H., Bynum, T., & Weisel, D. (1998). A tale of two cities: Gangs as organized crime groups. In J. Miller, C. L. Maxson, & M. W. Klein (Eds.), *The modern gang reader* (pp. 73–93). Los Angeles, CA: Roxbury Publishing.

Decker, S. H., & Chapman, M. T. (2008). *Drug smugglers on drug smuggling.* Philadelphia: Temple University Press.

Franklin, J., Paxson, V., Perrig, A., & Savage, S. (2007). *An inquiry into the nature and cause of the wealth of internet miscreants.* Paper presented at CCS07, October 29–November 2, 2007, Alexandria, VA.

Herley, C., & Florencio, D. (2010). Nobody sells gold for the price of silver: Dishonesty, uncertainty and the underground economy. In T. Moor, D. J. Pym, & C. Ioannidis (Eds.), *Economics of information security and privacy* (pp. 35–53). New York: Springer.

Holt, T. J. (2007). Subcultural evolution? Examining the influence of on- and offline experiences on deviant subcultures. *Deviant Behavior, 28,* 171–198.

Holt, T. J. (2009). Lone hacks or group cracks: Examining the social organization of computer hackers. In F. Smalleger & M. Pittaro (Eds.), *Crimes of the Internet* (pp. 336–355). Upper Saddle River, NJ: Pearson Prentice Hall.

Holt, T. J. (2013). Exploring the social organization and structure of stolen data markets. *Global Crime, 14,* 155–174.

Holt, T. J., & Blevins, K. R. (2007). Examining sex work from the client's perspective: Assessing johns using online data. *Deviant Behavior, 28,* 333–354.

Holt, T. J., & Lampke, E. (2010). Exploring stolen data markets on-line: Products and market forces. *Criminal Justice Studies, 23,* 33–50.

Holt, T. J., Strumsky, D., Smirnova, O., & Kilger, M. (2012). Examining the social networks of malware writers and hackers. *International Journal of Cyber Criminology, 6,* 891–903.

Holzman, H. R., & Pines, S. (1982). Buying sex: The phenomenology of being a John. *Deviant Behavior, 4*(1), 89–116.

Jacobs, B. (1996). Crack dealers apprehension avoidance techniques: A case of restrictive deterrence. *Criminology, 34,* 409–431.

Mann, D., & Sutton, M. (1998). Netcrime: More changes in the organisation of thieving. *British Journal of Criminology, 38,* 201–229.

Meyer, G. R. (1989). *The social organization of the computer underground.* Master's thesis, Northern Illinois University.

Milrod, C., & Weitzer, R. (2012). The intimacy prism: Emotion management among the clients of escorts. *Men and Masculinities, 15,* 447–467.

Motoyama, M., McCoy, D., Levchenko, K., Savage, S., & Voelker, G. M. (2011). An analysis of underground forums. *IMC'11,* 71–79.

Scott, M. S., & Dedel, K. (2006). Street prostitution. US Department of Justice, Office of Community Oriented Policing Services.

Sharp, K., & Earle, S. (2003). Cyberpunters and cyberwhores: Prostitution on the Internet. In Y. Jewkes (Ed.), *Dot Cons. Crime, deviance and identity on the Internet* (pp. 36–52). Portland, OR: Willan Publishing.

Wehinger, F. (2011). The Dark Net: Self-regulation dynamics of illegal online markets for identities and related services. *Intelligence and Security Informatics Conference,* 209–213.

CHAPTER 5

Visualizing the Networks of Economic Transactions and Ads in Stolen Data Markets

Abstract This chapter explores how social network analysis can enlighten our understanding of the deviant exchanges between data market participants at the global (network overall) and local (key players) levels. It starts with the network visualizations and global network measures. The correlations between user centrality (measure derived from the network) and the number of posts a user has made (measure collected from the forums) do not differentiate between ripping and non-ripping forums, but indicate a high variation among forums. On most forums, the sellers are central users, indicating their importance to the existence of the market, while the buyers create the most discussion. The chapter ends with Monte Carlo simulations of the networks attempting to identify their hidden structure.

Keywords Social network analysis • Density • Centrality • Resilience • Disruption

The previous chapter demonstrated that forum participants work at different levels of organizational complexity simultaneously (Best & Luckenbill, 1994). Chapter 2 showed the wide range of products, services, and countries affected by stolen data markets, while Chap. 3 established that both buyers and sellers may gain large revenues from the sale of information. Even a less experienced buyer, given certain level of luck, may earn substantial revenue from a minimal investment as long as the buyer is willing to face the risk of making multiple empty or invalid data purchases.

The preceding chapters focused on either the individual actor, product, or pricing as the unit of analyses, which is helpful to understand the social and economic dynamics of these markets. The public nature of the forums also establishes a unique opportunity to measure direct engagement and connections between participants based on the posts they make. The observed communications allow us to use social network analyses to visualize the exchanges made between forum actors, and better identify key players and their role within the market.

To that end, this chapter utilizes social network analysis techniques that have a long history of representing exchanges between various actors (Wasserman & Faust, 1994). This analytical technique allows both the visualization of users' communications, as well as the extraction of network connectivity to identify global patterns in the otherwise hidden networks of data market participants. In addition, social network analysis enables researchers to consider connections between participants based on their roles in both a forum and a thread. In turn, we can validate the findings from prior chapters related to the organizational composition of the markets, and attempt to identify differences between ripping and non-ripping forums on the basis of connectivity.

Social Network Analysis in Research on Stolen Data Markets

While the previous chapter considered social relationships based on the quotes and information posted by individuals, social network analyses considers connectivity based on the number of observable relationships between participants to understand the shape and composition of networks overall (e.g. Bakker, Raab, & Milward, 2012; Motoyama, McCoy, Levchenko, Savage, & Voelker, 2011; Yip, Webber, & Shadbolt, 2013). Such analyses are challenged by the fact that illicit markets, like those studied here, have a large number of connections between participants that are hidden from the general public. As a result, they may be viewed as a "dark network" because connections cannot be observed until the larger network has been dismantled or in some way disrupted (Bakker et al., 2012).

Bakker and colleagues (2012) proposed a theoretical approach to the study of dark networks by attempting to explain their resilience over time. Research on legitimate organizations suggests that they are able to survive the loss of key actors who link individuals or networks together because they are balanced in both resiliency and efficiency (Bakker et al., 2012). The network resiliency measures its capacity to withstand big shocks and rebound after key players' removal (Bakker et al., 2012), while its efficiency refers to how well the network can transmit information. Functional specialization reduces redundancy and increases efficiency. If this same dynamic can be observed in dark networks, then there must be some degree of labor differentiation between actors.

Actor differentiation creates opportunities for hierarchical structures, where individuals with different responsibilities can be managed through coordinated relationships in a top-down structure, similar to teams and formal organizations within the Best and Luckenbill (1994) framework. However, these benefits of efficiency are offset by the reduction in resiliency due to the hierarchical nature of operations. If a key player is removed within such a structure, all associated connections are removed as well which can dismantle the entire network. The most resilient dark networks are robust, as they will have the capacity to withhold strong shocks, and rebound after them (Bakker et al., 2012). Should a network seek to be robust, individuals must have a larger number of redundant relationships, so that lost connections can be replaced easily increasing the network's resiliency. However, this, in turn, will decrease the network's efficiency.

Researchers have applied this framework of social network analysis to various real-world offender groups (e.g. Bakker et al., 2012), as well as on-line relationships including gang members (Décary-Hétu & Morselli, 2011; Morselli & Décary Hétu, 2010; Womer & Bunker, 2010), hacker forums (Décary-Hétu & Dupont, 2012), as well as the social network profiles of malware writers and hackers (Holt, Strumsky, Smirnova, & Kilger, 2012). Few have used network analyses to examine stolen data forums whose findings suggest that individual threads within the forums are designed to facilitate sales transactions, often with a high degree of connectivity between buyers and interested parties (Motoyama et al., 2011; Yip et al., 2013). Buyers make a greater number of public posts relative to sellers (Motoyama et al., 2011; Yip et al., 2013), though seller connectivity appears to increase over time as buyers make contact with them to engage in a transaction. For example, Motoyama et al. (2011) found approximately 10 % of sellers across all of the sites account for almost 50 %

of all resources sold; this exemplifies how trust can have substantive impact on sellers' productivity. Unverified sellers appear to have a greater number of contacts in any given forum as they must communicate with more experienced members who understand the process of the market and are willing to take certain risks in order to engage in commerce (Yip et al., 2013).

Though prior research provides insight into the ways that network connectivity is influenced by an actor's role within the market, multiple questions remain regarding the networks that undergird these forums. It is unclear how sellers and buyers are positioned within markets of varying sizes and organizational sophistication. Furthermore, it is not clear how networks are shaped across a range of active markets. Such information can improve our knowledge of the market, and identify more effective tactics to disrupt the activities of buyers and sellers (Bakker et al., 2012).

SOCIAL NETWORK ANALYSES APPLIED TO STOLEN DATA MARKETS

Since social network analyses enable the visualization of users' communications and network connections, they are vital to understand network structures within and across all the forums. In this analysis, individual posters become network vertices (V), while their forum interactions (C) establish connections between them (Zhang, Ackerman, & Adamic, 2007). These relationships (C) and participants (V) identify a given network $N(V, C)$ where $C \subseteq V \times V$. It is important to note that an arc assumes that there is a specific direction in the flow of information between participants. In the case of forums, an arc may be created based on the assumption that conversation flows from the TS to the people who chose to participate in that thread. A tie does not assume a direction of information between participants. We use arcs in this analysis for the sake of consistent comparisons in the networks across all the forums included in this analysis.

Each individual forum thread can be viewed as information exchanges between different participants. If we view these exchanges collectively, we can build networks of forum activity. In the loner type of organization, the forums may be dominated by single ads. A single dot represents a user who started a thread that no one else engages in or that did not generate any visible activity within that thread. For example, Fig. 5.1a shows three users who posted their ads without anybody responding to them publically; hence, this figure represents three different threads.

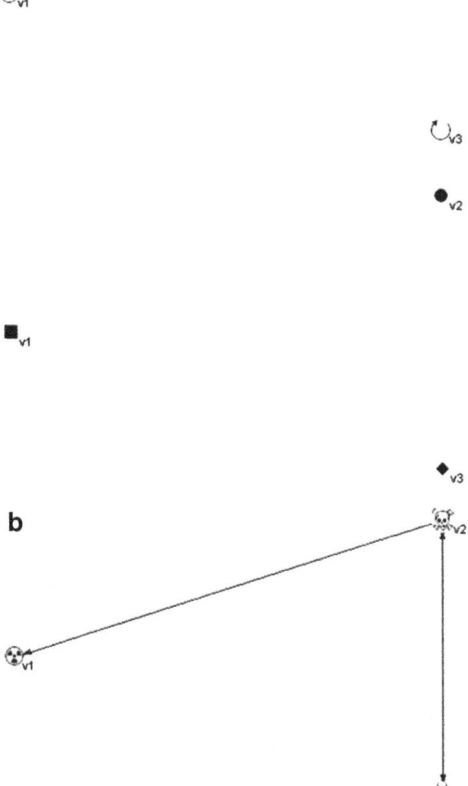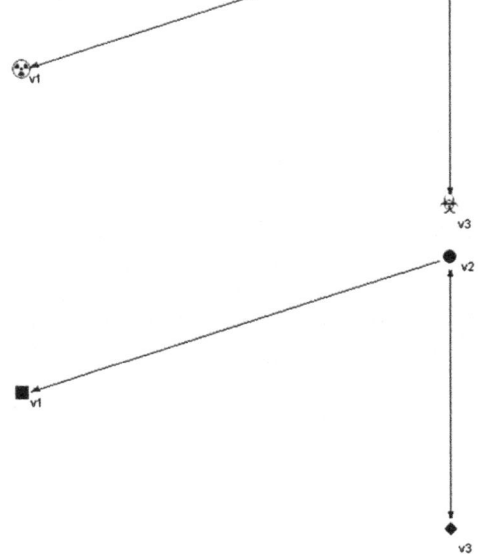

Fig. 5.1 (**a**) Network visualization of threads with no responses (3 users, 3 threads). (**b**) Network visualization of threads with replies (3 users, 2 threads)

In the event that an individual replies to his/her own post in a thread, it becomes a loop or self-reference. In threads where individuals respond to an initial post, the direction of arcs (connections between users) goes from the topic starter to the rest of the thread (see Fig. 5.1b), or from the ad to the people interested in the ad. These can be simple interactions or exchanges (Best & Luckenbill, 1994): question and answer, advertisement and response, or information offered–offer received. When the users continuously participate in multiple different threads, they connect these threads together in a larger network of criminal activities. That is, a user participating in multiple threads (e.g. either through buying or selling or providing additional feedback) connects each thread through his/her activities. This participation in multiple different threads indicates that this user may become familiar with the other users on the forum.

Due to the more or less public nature of this sample of forums, any user could see the content of any thread so long as they were either a registered user or able to find the forum through Google or another search engine. Additionally, this data set includes samples of threads from sub-forums, thus it is not representative of the entire sub-forum's participants. Furthermore, these networks do not include private exchanges in and out of the forums.

As a result, the findings presented here are only representative of a portion of the larger set of complete networks. Due to the difficulties in obtaining private exchanges between buyers and sellers in these markets, our networks focus on the public exchange of information. Even though some interactions on these forums may be random (e.g. buyers searching on-line for specific products, registering on various forums, and trying multiple venues for accessing the needed products), there will be a certain systematic component (e.g. a potential correlation between economic and forum activity). Thus, this analysis provides important initial insights into the surface-level network structures of these markets.

The network analyses can be broken down into two levels: global and local (de Nooy, Mrvar, & Batagelj, 2005). At the global level, the emergent properties of the networks can be extracted from all interactions within the network, showing how the network as a whole can be larger than the simple sum of its individual members. For example, we can calculate network density (the ratio of existing to potential ties) as one of the measures of how well the users are connected to each other. Global network measures are necessary to understand how the whole of a network varies from its individual parts, and identify additional properties that emerge from interactions with large number of people. At the local level, the individual characteristics of the network participants and their connections to their neighbors can be studied. For example, the users who participate in multiple popular threads will be more central to the distribution of the information on the network. In combination, the global and local levels of network analyses allow us to understand how the information about stolen data flows through the market.

Three major measures were calculated at the global level for each network in order to explore their resiliency, redundancy, and structure generally. First, network density was determined based on the ratio of existing ties to the number of all possible ties in the network. The higher the network density number, the higher the propensity of that network to transmit information between users (de Nooy et al., 2005).

Second, the average degree of connectivity was measured based on the average number of users that can be connected through the network. This measure identifies how far information can traverse a network through existing connections (de Nooy et al., 2005). Most networks that have higher than 1 average degree (e.g. where at least two users are connected) usually form a "giant component" where all participants are connected to one another (de Nooy et al., 2005). A component is a subset of network where each node is connected to one another. On one extreme, each thread may become a separate component (e.g. users post and reply only to separate threads), though at the other extreme, everyone could participate in all threads on the forum. Most of the networks in these forums lay between these extremes.

Finally, the all-degree centrality is calculated derived from the general connectedness of users on the network based on associations with others in threads (de Nooy et al., 2005). At the global level, this measure indicates the overall connectivity on the network. At the local level, this information allows for the identification of central users (de Nooy et al., 2005) who may be a point of leverage to disrupt the larger network if they were removed (Bakker et al., 2012). The measures were calculated for both directed networks, where information flows from the topic starter to participants in the thread, and undirected networks that assume everyone communicates with everyone.

Individual user-level measures were also calculated to compare against the global-level network measures. An all-degree centrality measure was calculated at the individual user level expressed as the proportion of vertices incident on a node from the total nodes on a network. Specifically, a user with the highest degree centrality will communicate with the largest number of other users on a forum. The local-level measures can be easily depicted on the networks, and visualized on the basis of categorical (aka partitions) and continuous (aka vectors) variables. For example, the size of each node can be scaled based on its centrality to understand the flow of information from central users to other participants (de Nooy et al., 2005, p. 113). In each forum, the total number of posts made by each user over the life of the forum is provided in some section, whether under the date of their current post or below their username. This detail is vital to understand their overall involvement in the forum beyond what is evident in the threads sampled here. The number of posts is treated as a vector and represented as different sized vertexes, where larger nodes represent a larger number of posts.

In the situation where the most central users are also frequent posters, for example, replying to a lot of threads to give feedback, or attempting to disrupt threads by posting their own advertisements, the centrality of a user (a measure derived from the network itself) will be highly correlated with the number of posts they make. This is a separate situation from instances where users connect to nodes (such as sellers) based on their reputation or knowledge. Sellers with a solid reputation might not need to make frequent posts in a forum to facilitate economic activity. Instead, they may be more active in ICQ and other messaging systems to interact with customers (Motoyama et al., 2011; Yip et al., 2013). Thus, Pearson correlation coefficients are calculated for each forum since both the number of posts and user centrality are continuous variables.

In addition, the users are partitioned on the basis of their expressed interest in buying data, selling a product, or exchanging information. Hence, we can visualize these economic activities on the networks. The neutral nodes have made posts not specifically related to buying, selling, or exchange, as defined in economic analysis section of this report. This is the broadest category as it captures both positive and negative comments, feedback by users, thread hijacking, and administrative interferences.

The basic composition of the forums limits our ability to determine certain characteristics about the networks. Since forums allow anyone who is a participant to observe exchanges in threads, the indirect flow of information may be greater than what is captured by the number of participants in a thread (Zhang et al., 2007). The fact that most purchases and exchanges take place outside of the forums also limits our ability to fully represent the network structures of participants.

The preliminary nature of these findings are, however, invaluable to identify any commonalities between these markets and other network structures in both legitimate (Zhang et al., 2007) and criminal groups alike (Bakker et al., 2012; Décary-Hétu & Dupont, 2012; Holt et al., 2012; Motoyama et al., 2011). The qualitative analysis of the posts' content presented in Chap. 4 allows us to identify the economic activity of users, while social network analyses presented here visualize who shares information about stolen data. It would seem plausible that individuals selling information would have a more central position on the network (see Motoyama et al., 2011), which can be examined through network measures of centrality.

LOW DENSITY AND NETWORK EFFICIENCY OF FORUMS

We begin with global-level analysis. Table 5.1 shows the summary information for the forums, such as number of different threads, different users, loops, multiple lines, multiple loops, and the percent of users in the largest component on the network. The loops represent the topic starter's attempts at either clarifying information initially posted or updating the thread to attract more attention. The multiple lines identify several comments by various users and/or participation of these users in different threads together. The presence of multiple lines, loops, and multiple loops

Table 5.1 Network metrics by forum

Forum	Number of threads	Number of users	Number of total arcs	Number of single loops	Number of multiple lines	Number of multiple loops	Percent in the largest component
1	55	81	104	55	0	7	18.5
2	128	160	333	126	36	25	86.25
4	144	170	645	345	328	225	50.59
5	89	88	93	86	0	9	4.54
6	48	416	342	47	0	8	58.89
7	202	157	375	202	13	134	71.98
8	590	471	1219	278	121	470	55.29
9	312	650	1076	286	2	26	73.69
10	35	66	178	33	10	85	60.61
11	60	237	573	40	85	56	97.01
12	71	119	169	53	3	18	62.19
13	153	293	481	127	23	113	55.63

complicates the computation of certain network measures. For example, clustering coefficients can be computed only for the networks without multiple lines or loops. The largest component indicates the area on the network where all users are connected to each other.

The findings suggest substantive variation in the nature of forums. In Forums 1 and 5, users may not know one another due to the lack of interactions, and the presence of self-loops by the TS. These forums also have a very small "largest component," representing the component of the network where different forum participants connect together through various threads. There are also a number of forums (e.g. Forums 7 and 8) where there is more conversation and engagement between participants. These forums may demonstrate the social learning process evident in general interest hacker forums (e.g. Holt et al., 2012) and on-line networks (Zhang et al., 2007).

Table 5.2 represents the global measures, including network density, average degree, and all-degree centralization. The higher the network density, the better the network can transmit information between users (de Nooy et al., 2005). The average degree of connectivity measures how far the information can traverse the network. The all-degree centralization is calculated as the variation in the number of lines incident on each node (node degree) over the maximum degree variation for the network of a given size (de Nooy et al., 2005).

Table 5.2 Network density and centrality metrics by forum

Forum	Original network		No loops, no multiple lines		
	Network density	Average degree	Network density	Average degree	All-degree centralization
1	0.016	2.568	0.008	1.210	2.456
2	0.013	4.163	0.008	2.450	35.215
4	0.023	7.741	0.007	2.471	18.482
5	0.012	2.114	0.001	0.159	1.453
6	0.002	1.644	0.002	1.418	45.007
7	0.015	4.777	0.007	2.038	8.084
8	0.006	5.266	0.002	1.512	22.843
9	0.003	3.346	0.002	2.345	26.409
10	0.010	4.835	0.007	3.308	33.630
11	0.041	5.394	0.012	1.515	5.406
12	0.012	2.840	0.007	1.597	8.850
13	0.006	3.283	0.003	1.488	18.885

The majority of forums have low network density, suggesting actors recycle some information. These redundancies slow the spread of new information, whether data or services, while at the same time making it difficult to disrupt the network through the removal of one or two sellers. The network redundancy may make the network less efficient while making the networks more resilient (see Bakker et al., 2012). For example, the sale of the same dumps or CVV data may artificially increase the supply of data, but increase the probability that a given sale may be rendered non-usable to a buyer. This may create greater opportunities for the proliferation of rippers within a market (see Chap. 3), which would lead buyers to discount all sale prices including those from legitimate sellers. In turn, this may lead to decreased profits for both sellers and buyers.

For certain global network measures, we have to remove loops and multiple lines (e.g. network clustering coefficients or all-degree centralization). The removal of loops and multiple lines also drastically decreases the density and average connectivity between users. Overall, the users tend to update their ads frequently (creating self-loops) and exchange a lot of posts with the same users over one or multiple threads.

In light of the low density evident across these forums, it appears that they are inefficient at the distribution of knowledge and information due to multiple redundancies. The myriad data sellers and service providers demonstrate that removing a single individual from the network will have no true impact on the network as a whole. Others can easily replace that individual seller or actor, and maintain the general status of the market (see also Motoyama et al., 2011). This is particularly evident in Forum 8, which is one of the two ripping forums within this sample. There is a large number of different users and isolates where no one has replied to the originating post in the thread. This suggests that there are minimal replies to any post (Herley & Florencio, 2010). This may be due to the ripping or fraudulent information disintegrating the network structure of the forum.

The other ripping forum, Forum 2, has a smaller number of posts and a high average degree, indicating a higher number of replies to any post made and greater user interactions. Over 80 % of participants in this sample of threads from Forum 2 communicate with each other compared to about 50 % in Forum 8. Overall, there were no consistent differences observed between ripping and non-ripping forums based on network measures. This may stem from the different time frames sampled across these two ripping forums: Forum 8 had posts starting in February 2009, while Forum 2 began in December 2010. Forum 2 may be in the initial phases of its development and have less reputation or recognition among users relative to the more established population in Forum 8. Thus, it is possible that as rippers become more active in Forum 2, the communication between users may decrease, leading to a larger proportion of isolates over time as the negative consequences of ripping affect the users (Herley & Florencio, 2010; Wehinger, 2011).

NETWORK COMPONENTS

To further understand the network structures of these forums, they can be broken down into individual components. An individual component on the network is the area of where each user can be connected to one another. In our sample, some forums have a large component where a majority of nodes are connected through their participation in different threads (see Table 5.1). The individual components are formed by including both strong and weak ties between participants; the users participating in multiple threads form the center of these components. Weak ties might have less redundant information and form bridges between more connected components of the network (Granovetter, 1973). Three non-ripping forums in this sample (Forums 7, 9, and 11) have more than 70 % of all nodes connected through various threads. Users in these forums may be more familiar with one another and therefore operate in a more insulated network with reduced risk of compromise (see Herley & Florencio, 2010; Wehinger, 2011). Thus, mutual participation in various threads can actually enhance certain users' reputations as being reliable sellers.

Examining this sample of forums suggests that Forum 5 has very little connectivity, with the average degree influenced by the only component formed on this network. This forum provides an example of the situation where everyone "talks" past one another; that is, nearly every user forms his/her own thread with minimal participation in other threads. This can be an example of multiple sellers operating on the forum. In such situation, our calculations will most likely omit any profits that such networks can still generate (e.g. through the personal communication not observable by the researchers).

At the same time, the forum with the largest number of threads in this sample (Forum 8) is also a ripping forum. Compared to other forums with over 400 users, this forum has the lowest percentage of users in the main component. This disconnect between users may be a reflection of ripping, as individuals may create identities just to post ads and cheat others (see

Herley & Florencio, 2010; Wehinger, 2011). This provides support for the assertion that ripping markets may have limited ties between users while reputable forums have stronger connections between users which help to establish user reputations (Motoyama et al., 2011). This further reinforces the concept of multiple markets operating on-line to sell data with varying degrees of trust and user insularity (Herley & Florencio, 2010; Wehinger, 2011).

VISUALIZING ECONOMIC ACTIVITY AND CENTRALITY

The advantage of network analysis includes visualizations of stolen data and service information spread. There are two types of measures that can be depicted on the networks: measures derived from the networks (e.g. centrality of individual nodes) and those collected with the data (e.g. economic activity of the users). The centrality of each user is determined by the number of users that an individual is connected to. In essence, network centrality identifies those users who participate in the threads with the highest overall participation. This is local-level analysis. Data sellers would seem to be the most logical candidates for the most central user positions on the network. However, since the formed network represents the public interactions by the users, the buyers may generate more information as they are trying to separate the sellers of working stolen data from the rippers.

To understand these issues more completely, we analyzed the economic and forum activity of the users, with the exception of Forum 3 due to its small sample size. The total number of posts becomes a proxy for the overall activity of a user in any given forum. Economic activity identifies whether the user posted on buying, selling, or exchanging the stolen data. If users only participated in the general discussions, then such users are identified as neutral (none of the economic activity detected). Some users may be both buying and selling in different threads. The majority of users, however, had only one economic code associated with their name. The legend in each graph reflects the following relationships: sales = squares, buying = circles, exchange = stars, both buying and selling = hazard symbol, and neutral = no symbol.

Each figure separates components by their size to identify the activity happening in the most connected sectors of the networks. For each forum, we create two figures: the economic activity by the users' centrality and economic activity by the number of posts each user made. We also calculated the Pearson correlation coefficient between the number of posts by the user (a measure collected from the data) and user centrality (a measure created from the networks). Since the number of posts indicates how often a given user attempts to interact with other forum participants, the correlation coefficient measures whether the most central users are also the users who generate the most posts.

For Forum 1, all the users are recorded as neutral on the forum (see Fig. 5.2a). The node size in the Fig. 5.2a differs with their centrality. The smallest nodes do not have any other nodes connecting them, and usually represented by single dots, or isolates. The information that these users provide may still flow through the network as others may still read it. However, this information does not generate interactions between the users in the same fashion that information flows between the users in the

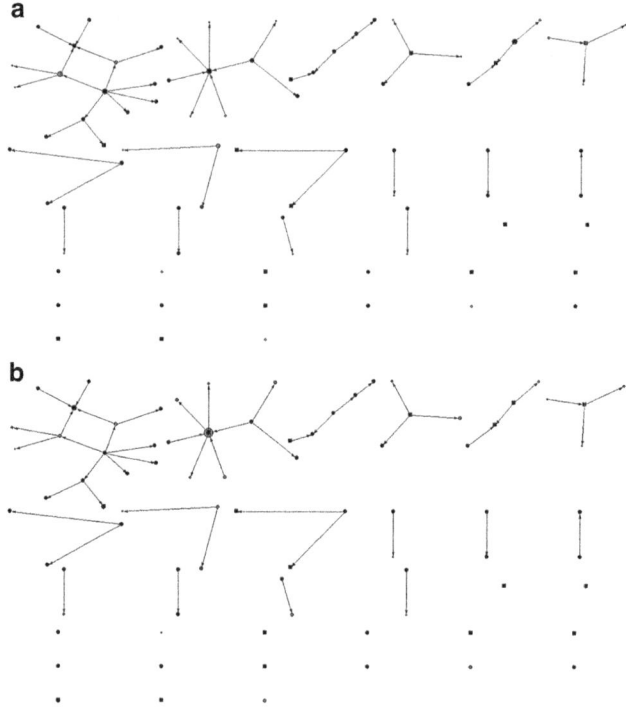

Fig. 5.2 (a) Forum 1 economic activity by centrality. (b) Forum 1 economic activity by number of posts. *Notes*: Each node is a user. The network is separated in individual connected components, some of which may contain multiple threads.

connected components. Some users may increase their centrality through self-promotion and self-reference; that is, continuously updating and keeping their own threads active. In Fig. 5.2b the isolates' sizes differ by the number of posts they created. The number of posts and the user's centrality (a proportion of nodes incident on the node under study from all nodes on the network) are significantly correlated with each other with a Pearson correlation (r) of 0.5 ($p < 0.001$), suggesting that a node's centrality is correlated with the frequency of a participant's posts in this forum.

In the Forum 2, the sellers are more central (see Fig. 5.3a), while the buyers and neutral users post more often (see Fig. 5.3b). Neutral users appear to be the most important hubs for network connectivity overall, suggesting that they are key players within this forum. There is also very

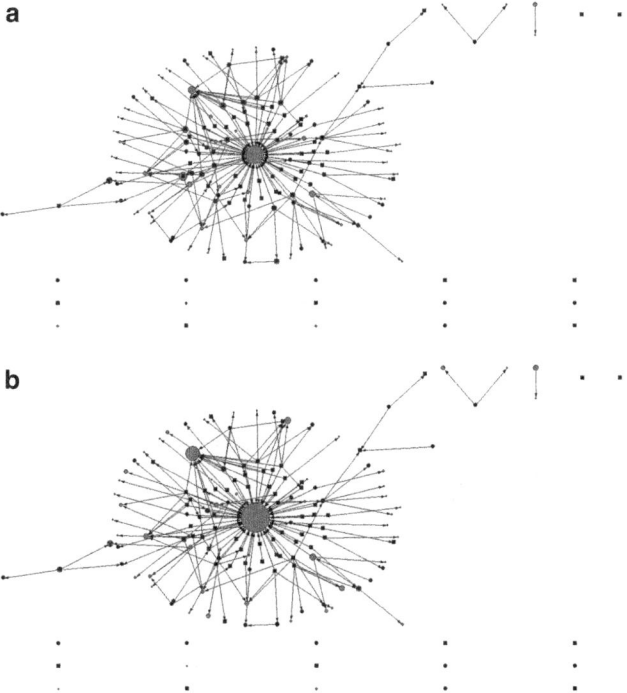

Fig. 5.3 (a) Forum 2 economic activity by centrality. (b) Forum 2 economic activity by number of posts. *Notes*: Each node is a user. The network is separated in individual connected components, some of which may contain multiple threads.

high correlation between the number of posts and users' centrality (0.935, $p<0.001$). This forum is one of the two ripping forums in this sample, which may account for this relationship as neutral users are critical to help identify who are rippers.

Forum 4, on the other hand, shows a modest correlation coefficient between centrality and the number of posts ($r=0.398$; $p<0.05$; see Figs. 5.4a and b). But it also illustrates that sellers are central to this forum despite the fact that neutral users or buyers create a larger number of posts (see also Motoyama et al., 2011; Yip et al., 2013).

Forum 5 visualization demonstrates a large number of isolates (Figs. 5.5a and b). There is no correlation between the number of posts and the user's centrality ($r=0.06$; $p>0.05$). Only one of the sellers (large green isolate) becomes more visible on the network based on the number of

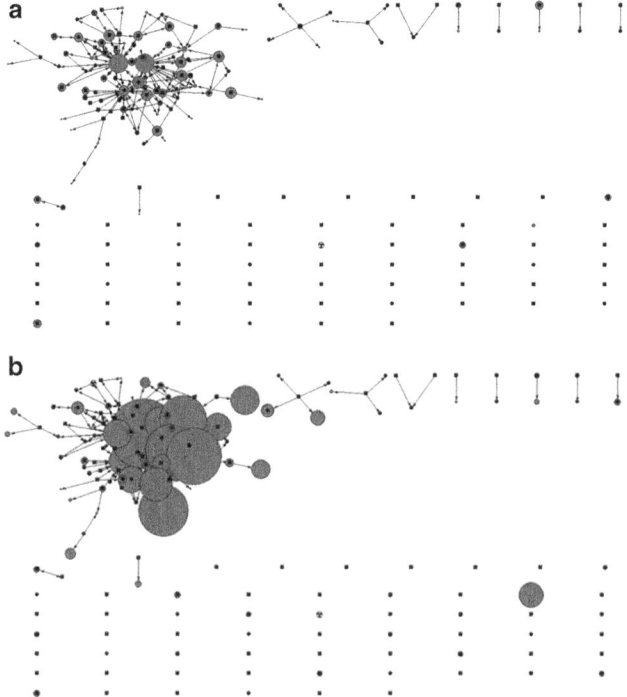

Fig. 5.4 (a) Forum 4 economic activity by centrality. (b) Forum 4 economic activity by number of posts. *Notes*: Each node is a user. The network is separated in individual connected components, some of which may contain multiple threads.

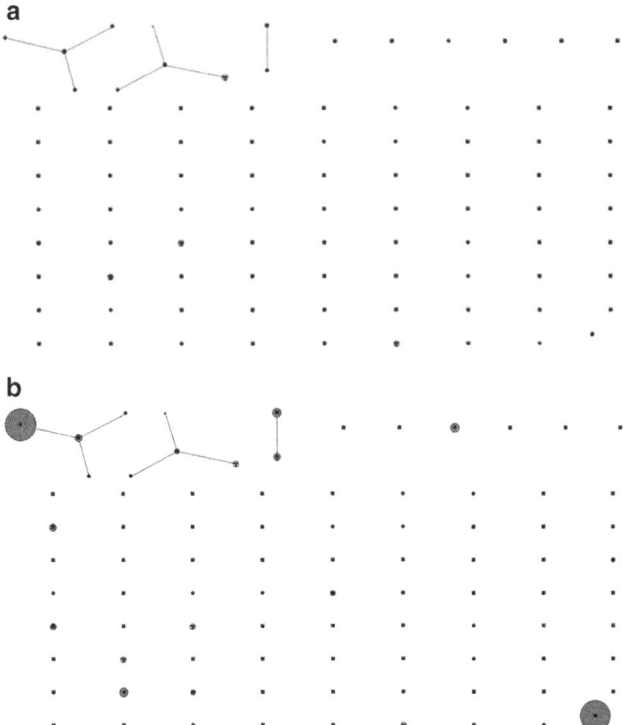

Fig. 5.5 (a) Forum 5 economic activity by centrality. (b) Forum 5 economic activity by number of posts. *Notes:* Each node is a user. The network is separated in individual connected components, some of which may contain multiple threads.

posts (comparing Figs. 5.5a and b). This may illustrate the self-promotion by the seller. This forum is saturated with a lot of sales.

Forum 6 again demonstrates that buyers post frequently, while sellers are more central in the network. There is no significant correlation between the frequency of posts and the number of other nodes this user is connected to in this forum ($r=0.067$; $p>0.05$). The one user who both buys and sells products is both central and relatively "vocal" on the network (Figs. 5.6a and b).

Forum 7 has 157 users which is more than some of the other forums sampled, united in 202 threads, and is a more connected network overall (see Figs. 5.7a and b). It is one of the three forums that has the larger number of threads than users. The number of posts and users' centrality are correlated at $r=0.457$ ($p<0.001$).

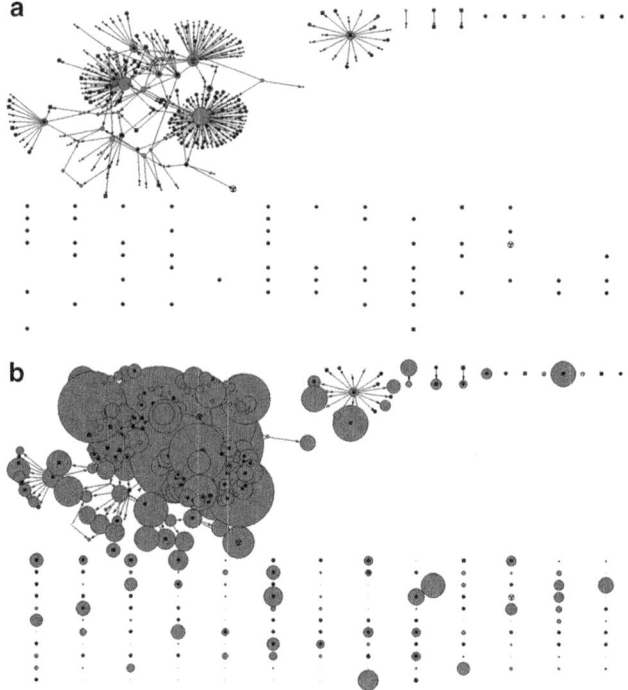

Fig. 5.6 (a) Forum 6 economic activity by centrality. (b) Forum 6 economic activity by number of posts. *Notes*: Each node is a user. The network is separated in individual connected components, some of which may contain multiple threads.

Forum 8 visualizations, one of the two ripping forums, suggest that there are a large number of sellers present (see Figs. 5.8a and b). The sellers in this site are also more central than other users, but unlike another ripping forum, the centrality on this forum is not correlated with the number of posts a user makes ($r=0.15$; $p<0.05$).

The Forum 9 network again suggests that neutral users and buyers create a larger number of posts, while sellers are more central (see Figs. 5.9a and b). At the same time, the correlation between the number of posts and the centrality of users is relatively high at $r=0.74$ ($p<0.001$).

Forum 10 was relatively smaller compared to the other forums in this sample as it had only 66 users (see Figs. 5.10a and b). This forum, however, had a largest average degree of connectivity at 3.308 (calculated

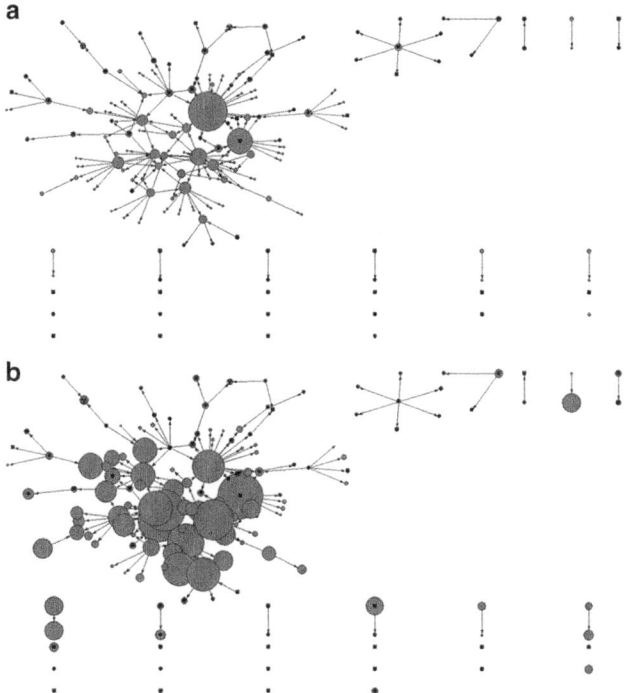

Fig. 5.7 (a) Forum 7 economic activity by centrality. (b) Forum 7 economic activity by number of posts. *Notes*: Each node is a user. The network is separated in individual connected components, some of which may contain multiple threads.

when we drop multiple lines and loops); on an average, about three users could be connected on this network. The number of posts and centrality are not correlated in this forum ($r = -0.11$; $p => 0.05$)

Forum 11 is characterized by an emergent "giant component" where 97% of forum users can be connected with each other through threads (see Figs. 5.11a and b). Unlike the previous forums, the most central users are neutral posters in this forum. This forum also registers a relatively rare economic activity—exchange (an isolate). This may be due to the fact that most of this forum population discussed methods and practices to facilitate the acquisition or sale of data, rather than the actual sale of products and services. This network may share more in common with traditional hacker forums (e.g. Décary-Hétu & Dupont, 2012) rather than the stolen

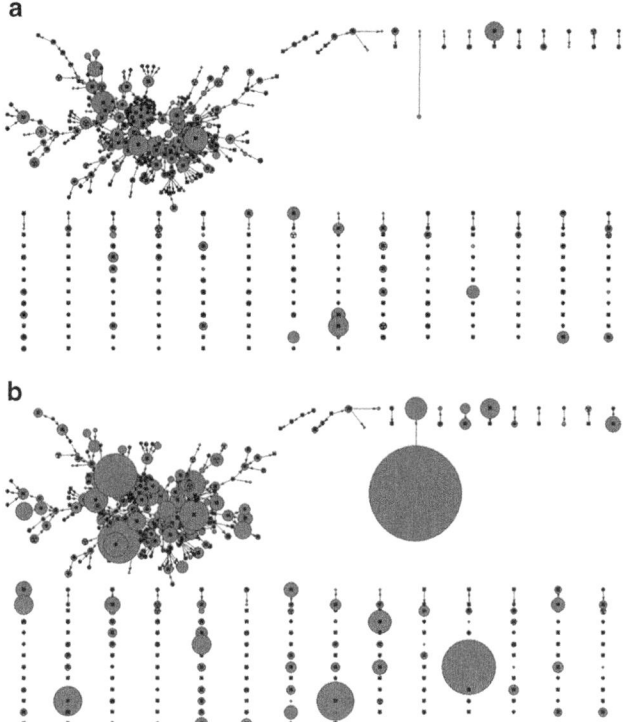

Fig. 5.8 (a) Forum 8 economic activity by centrality. (b) Forum 8 economic activity by number of posts. *Notes*: Each node is a user. The network is separated in individual connected components, some of which may contain multiple threads.

data markets previously presented. The correlation between users' centrality and the number of posts is $r = 0.46$ ($p < 0.001$).

Forum 12 is more heavily engaged in the sale of data with a very low Pearson correlation coefficient between users' centrality and the number of posts ($r = -0.009$; $p < 0.05$). In this network, two neutral users have the greatest centrality, followed by sellers, though neutral users had the largest proportion of posts overall (see Figs. 5.12a and b).

The final forum in this sample, Forum 13, conforms to the larger pattern of sellers being the most central actors within each forum, with buyers and neutral players posting more frequently (see Figs. 5.13a and b). There are also a number of isolates evident, regardless of their role in the economy of the site ($r = 0.04$; $p < 0.05$).

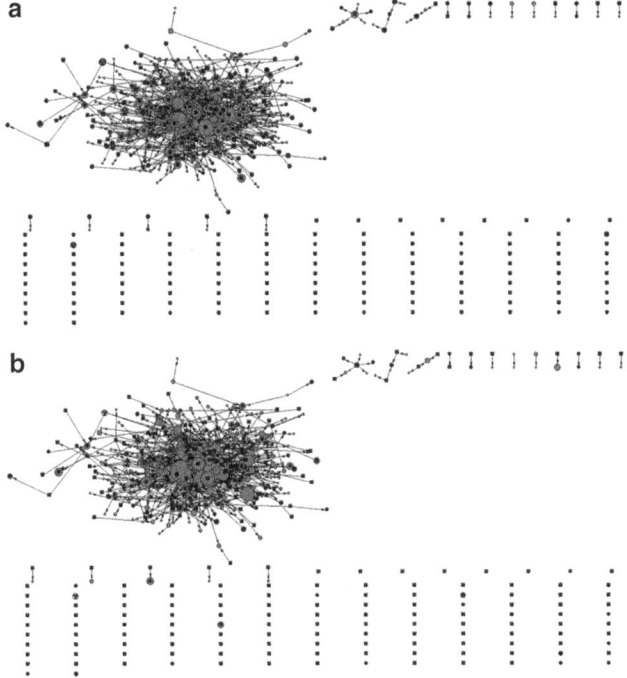

Fig. 5.9 (a) Forum 9 economic activity by centrality. (b) Forum 9 economic activity by number of posts. *Notes:* Each node is a user. The network is separated in individual connected components, some of which may contain multiple threads.

As a whole, the visualizations of centrality and economic activity demonstrate two issues. First, neutral users in the market are a critical resource to communicate normative values to others. Sellers offer stolen data and services that engender cybercrimes which drive the market, but the users who ask questions, provide feedback, or engage others help to disseminate information about individual reputation and the general norms of the market. This provides additional support for the qualitative finding that the market is participatory in nature (see Holt, 2013). Second, the lack of strong connections between participants also demonstrates that the market is collegial in nature rather than highly structured (Best & Luckenbill, 1994). Sellers are central hubs in some networks or isolates in others despite not making as many posts in keeping with the J-curve

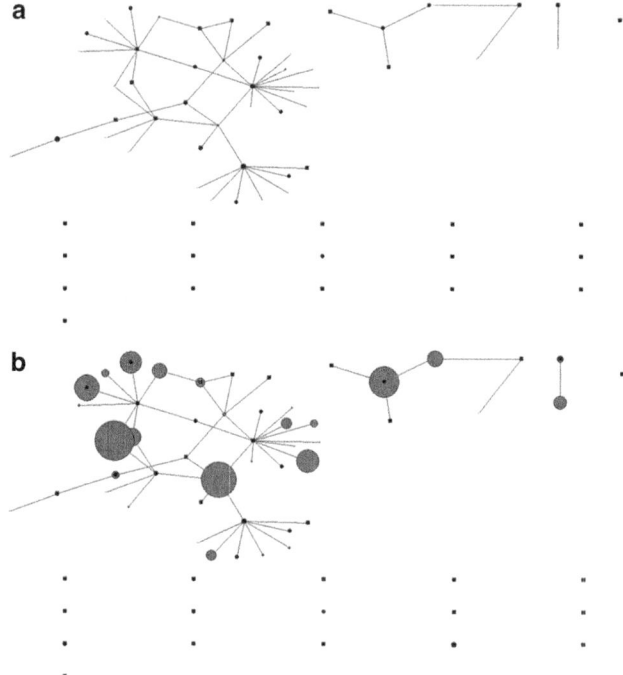

Fig. 5.10 (a) Forum 10 economic activity by centrality. (b) Forum 10 economic activity by number of posts. *Notes:* Each node is a user. The network is separated in individual connected components, some of which may contain multiple threads.

relationship observed in other research (Herring, 2004; Holt, 2009; Holt & Blevins, 2007; Robinson, 1984).

The low correlations between centrality and the number of posts indicate that in some forums, users do not become central based on the number of the posts they make. On some forums, the frequency with which a user posts in response to a thread is vital to their centrality.

STOLEN DATA MARKET STRUCTURE

Though the visualizations presented symbolize the observable part of the underlining structure of the stolen data market, there is a need to understand whether they have occurred randomly or more systematically.

VISUALIZING THE NETWORKS OF ECONOMIC TRANSACTIONS AND ADS... 119

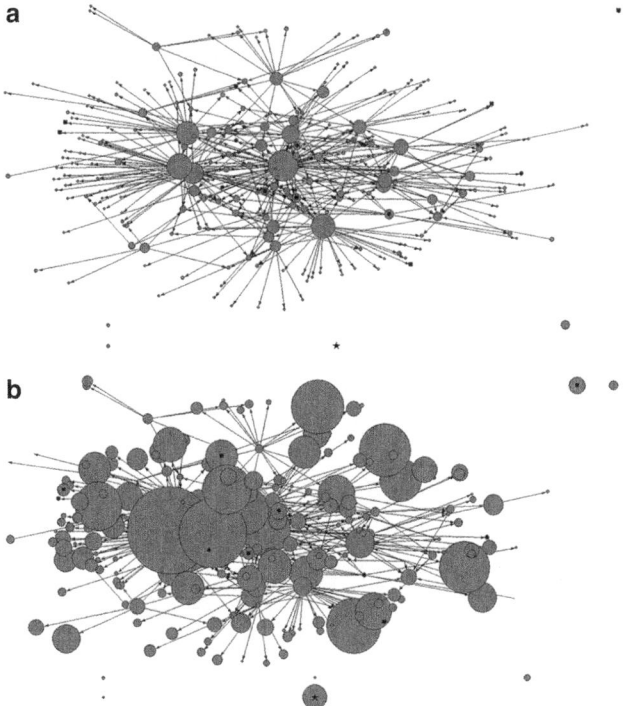

Fig. 5.11 (a) Forum 11 economic activity by centrality. (b) Forum 11 economic activity by number of posts. *Notes*: Each node is a user. The network is separated in individual connected components, some of which may contain multiple threads.

Identifying the forming mechanisms for stolen data markets can provide essential value for policy solutions, as they speak to general nature of how to dismantle the networks. If the studied forums exhibit characteristics of a random network, then the underlining mechanisms that form the actual network may be in some way similar to a simulated network (de Nooy et al., 2005), and may help our understanding of the stolen data market. If forums are created at random, and the participants comment on the posts (or make ads) randomly, then eliminating certain number of nodes can be a viable policy. On the other hand, in scale-free networks, the users with the most connections (e.g. sellers whose ads attract the most public discussions on the forum) will become hubs of the informational exchange

120   DATA THIEVES IN ACTION

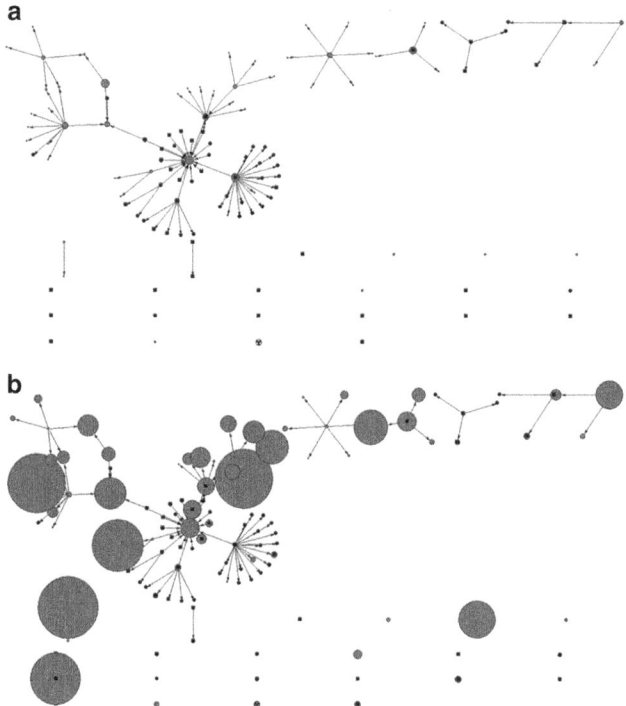

Fig. 5.12 (a) Forum 12 economic activity by centrality. (b) Forum 12 economic activity by number of posts. *Notes:* Each node is a user. The network is separated in individual connected components, some of which may contain multiple threads.

on the network. Hence, the focused disruption of such hubs may be helpful for the overall disruption of the network.

There are three major classes of random networks models that are tested here: classic uniform (e.g. Bernoulli), Small World (e.g. Watts–Strogatz models), and preferential attachment models. In the classic uniform random networks, all buyers and sellers have the same probability to participate in same threads, and they are likely to have the same number of links. In other words, the buyers randomly select a thread in a forum where they are going to buy products (a highly unlikely assumption). Such models do not allow loops, hence they cannot replicate the actually observed networks. Also, the assumption that buyers and sellers can randomly post in different threads ran contrary to the contextual analysis of the posts. But

VISUALIZING THE NETWORKS OF ECONOMIC TRANSACTIONS AND ADS... 121

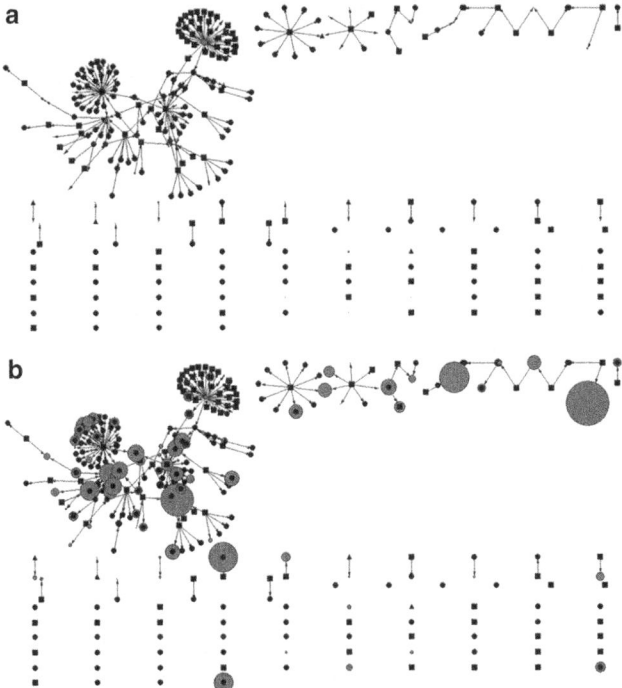

Fig. 5.13 (a) Forum 13 economic activity by centrality. (b) Forum 13 economic activity by number of posts. *Notes:* Each node is a user. The network is separated in individual connected components, some of which may contain multiple threads.

it is a good starting point as it can be expected that none of the classic uniform models will have similar parameters to observed forums.

The Small World model improves on the classical uniform models by introducing the concept that individuals will tend to be connected with their neighbors' neighbors. In stolen data markets, users may be after the same information and more likely to participate in the same threads. The Small World models combine the characteristics of the uniform random models such as path lengths with the higher clustering, which is frequently observed in the real networks. Taking a highly interconnected network, and randomly reconnecting (rewiring) some vertices to their neighbors, one can drastically reduce the diameter of such a network. As a result, this class of models is closer to many real-world networks.

However, Small World models do not usually have directionality, and hence lose one component of our actual networks. The rewiring probability can vary, but usually ranges between 0.1 and 0.5 (de Nooy et al., 2005) to produce the results closest to the observed networks. This range generates the Small World random models with the most similarity to the observed forums, but they are still significantly different.

Finally, preferential attachment models were conducted, that assume the vertices "prefer" to connect to nodes with the high degree or larger number of connections. Both sellers and buyers would prefer to participate in the same threads or reply to the posts of the most popular users. Such models usually replicate the commonly observed situation in actual networks where a small number of vertices have the most links. The preferential attachment models also have the probability of forming a tie (as in Small World models), along with two additional parameters, alpha (the preference for users to connect to other users with high indegree or those who participate in most threads) and beta (the preference of users to connect to other users with high outdegree or those who start the most threads). That is, a seller who starts a lot of threads will have a higher outdegree compared to the buyer who posts a lot of replies to other people's threads in the forum. We have used the probability of 0.5; alpha (indegree) equal to 0.25, and beta (outdegree) equal to 0.20. These parameters produce the results closest to our real networks.

Since each randomly generated model can have different parameters, we have run Monte Carlo simulations where we have created 100 different models for each forum, or 1300 random networks for each class of models (for the total of 3900 models).[1]

We start with the classical uniform models, and Table 5.3 compares the randomly generated networks using Monte Carlo simulations with the sampled networks. The results compare a random uniform network with the same number of users.

There are two density measures calculated, one that allows loops (density 1), and one without loops (density 2). We also calculate the average degree, network diameter, Watts–Strogatz clustering coefficient, and network clustering coefficient (transitivity). On an average, the randomly generated networks are denser (more connected) compared to the stolen data markets. They usually form nearly twice the number of connections between the users. The diameter of a given network is the longest of the shortest paths between the vertices in a network (the shortest distance between all vertices is calculated, and then the longest number among

Table 5.3 Directed Bernoulli random networks (the averages are for 100 random networks generated for each forum)

	Number of vertices	Number of lines	Loops	Multiple lines	Density 1	Density 2	Average degree	Diameter	Watts–Strogatz clustering coefficient	Network clustering coefficient (transitivity)
Forum 1	81	104	55	7	0.0159	0.0000	2.5679	2.0000	0.0000	0.0000
Average RM	81	208	0	0	0.0316	0.0320	5.1257	11.0571	0.0332	0.0325
Forum 2	160	333	126	36	0.0130	0.0000	4.1625	3.0000	0.0773	0.0079
Average RM	160	663	0	0	0.0259	0.0261	8.2894	8.0396	0.0268	0.0265
Forum 3	7	7	6	0	0.1429	0.0000	2.0000	1.0000	0.0000	0.0000
Average RM	7	14	0	0	0.2937	0.3426	4.1114	3.6436	0.3528	0.3188
Forum 4	170	658	345	328	0.0228	0.0000	7.7412	5.0000	0.4379	0.1333
Average RM	170	1317	0	0	0.0456	0.0458	15.4971	5.0200	0.0459	0.0458
Forum 5	88	93	86	9	0.0120	0.0000	2.1136	1.0000	0.0000	0.0000
Average RM	88	187	0	0	0.0241	0.0244	4.2450	13.4200	0.0241	0.0238
Forum 6	416	342	47	8	0.0020	0.0000	1.6442	4.0000	0.0392	0.0014
Average RM	416	685	0	0	0.0040	0.0040	3.2919	26.2600	0.0038	0.0038
Forum 7	157	375	202	147	0.0152	0.0000	4.7771	7.0000	0.0409	0.0245
Average RM	157	749	0	0	0.0304	0.0306	9.5443	7.2500	0.0305	0.0305
Forum 8	463	1219	748	591	0.00568646	0.0000	5.2657	3.0000	0.0029	0.0014

(continued)

Table 5.3 (continued)

	Number of vertices	Number of lines	Number of Loops	Multiple lines	Density 1	Density 2	Average degree	Diameter	Watts–Strogatz clustering coefficient	Network clustering coefficient (transitivity)
Average RM	463	2439	0	0	0.0114	0.0114	10.5362	8.0400	0.0115	0.0115
Forum 9	650	1076	312	28	0.0025	0.0000	3.3108	8.0000	0.0253	0.0093
Average RM	650	2159	0	0	0.0051	0.0051	6.6436	12.5300	0.0051	0.0051
Forum 10	66	178	118	95	0.0409	0.0000	5.3939	2.0000	0.0422	0.0089
Average RM	66	354	0	0	0.0814	0.0826	10.7391	5.3800	0.0832	0.0824
Forum 11	237	573	96	141	0.0102	0.0000	4.8354	5.0000	0.1361	0.0241
Average RM	237	1150	0	0	0.0205	0.0206	9.7029	7.6400	0.0204	0.0202
Forum 12	119	169	71	21	0.0119	0.0000	2.8403	2.0000	0.0247	0.0040
Average RM	119	339	0	0	0.0239	0.0241	5.6904	10.9100	0.0243	0.0239
Forum 13	293	481	240	136	0.0056	0.0000	3.2833	3.0000	0.0112	0.0007
Average RM	293	960	0	0	0.0112	0.0112	6.5525	11.2700	0.0111	0.0112

these shortest distances becomes the network diameter). While our networks usually have the diameters of 3 (Forum 12) or 4 (Forum 11); the random networks with the same number of vertices have double the diameter (connect more users). Watts–Strogatz clustering coefficient measures whether vertices tend to cluster together. For the forums, 2, 4, 6, 7, 9, and 11, the clustering coefficient of the actual network is higher than the randomly generated models. The other networks are sparser than the randomly generated networks. For forums 10 and 12, the Watts–Strogatz clustering coefficients are relatively close to the generated scale-free random networks (the z-scores for real networks are 2.01 and 2.64, respectively). This means that they are still significantly different at $p < 0.05$ level. None of the randomly generated networks recreated the loops or multiple lines in the observed networks. All observed models' parameters have z-scores ranging from 5 to 15, indicating that these classical models really cannot replicate the stolen data market formation.

Next we run Small World Monte Carlo simulations on. The results in Table 5.4 demonstrate that the model has difficulty reproducing the loops and multiple lines as well as directionality of our models.

Assuming normal distribution for the network parameters across all simulations, we are able to run a simple z-score test on whether our real networks' parameters can belong to this class of models. Some of the forums have z-scores in the range of $2-3^2$ for this class of random models (that is still outside of 68–95% of the data); hence the Small World model is a little bit closer to the sampled forums than the classical uniform model. For example, the Small World models have smaller diameters, which make this measure closer to our actual networks. However, almost all generated networks have higher clustering coefficients than observed data.

Finally, the preferential attachment models are represented in Table 5.5.

The simulated networks had higher densities than the actual networks and larger core components. The key differences suggest that certain underlying mechanisms make the networks of stolen data markets relatively unconnected while at the same time maintain the centrality of some sellers/buyers. Hence, we have a situation where stolen goods data markets are not as connected (e.g. as measured by average degree) as some other on-line networks (Adamic & Glance, 2005). And they exhibit characteristics similar to the J-curve of forum participation overall (e.g. Holt, 2007), that certain nodes collect the most links or hubs.

Since the observed networks could not be randomly generated and are most likely a reflection of underlining dark network processes, further

126 DATA THIEVES IN ACTION

Table 5.4 Undirected Small World random networks (the averages are for 100 random networks generated for each forum)

	Number of vertices	Number of lines	Loops	Multiple lines	Density 1	Density 2	Average degree	Diameter	Watts–Strogatz clustering coefficient	Network clustering coefficient (transitivity)
Forum 1	81	104	55	7	0.0159	0.0000	2.5679	2.0000	0.0000	0.0000
Average SW	81	162	0	0	0.0494	0.0500	4.0000	6.8400	0.1052	0.0910
Forum 2	160	333	126	36	0.0130	0.0000	4.1625	3.0000	0.0773	0.0079
Average SW	160	320	0	0	0.0250	0.0252	4.0000	8.1089	0.0819	0.0703
Forum 3	7	7	6	0	0.1429	0.0000	2.0000	1.0000	0.0000	0.0000
Average SW	7	14	0	0	0.5714	0.6667	4.0000	2.0396	0.6458	0.6145
Forum 4	170	658	345	328	0.0228	0.0000	7.7412	5.0000	0.4379	0.1333
Average SW	170	340	0	0	0.0456	0.0458	15.4971	8.2900	0.0235	0.0237
Forum 5	88	93	86	9	0.0120	0.0000	2.1136	1.0000	0.0000	0.0000
Average SW	88	187	0	0	0.0241	0.0244	4.2450	13.4200	0.0829	0.0684
Forum 6	416	342	47	8	0.0020	0.0000	1.6442	4.0000	0.0392	0.0014
Average SW	416	832	0	0	0.0096	0.0096	4.0000	9.7300	0.0701	0.0564
Forum 7	157	375	202	147	0.0152	0.0000	4.7771	7.0000	0.0409	0.0245
Average SW	157	314	0	0	0.0255	0.0256	4.0000	8.1500	0.0857	0.0708
Forum 8	463	1219	748	591	0.00568646	0.0000	5.2657	3.0000	0.0029	0.0014
Average SW	463	926	0	0	0.0086	0.0087	4.0000	9.9400	0.0712	0.0567
Forum 9	650	1076	312	28	0.0025	0.0000	3.3108	8.0000	0.0253	0.0093
Average SW	650	1300	0	0	0.0062	0.0062	4.0000	10.5600	0.0681	0.0541
Forum 10	66	178	118	95	0.0409	0.0000	5.3939	2.0000	0.0422	0.0089
Average SW	66	132	0	0	0.0606	0.0615	4.0000	6.6200	0.1139	0.0992
Forum 11	237	573	96	141	0.0102	0.0000	4.8354	5.0000	0.1361	0.0241
Average SW	237	474	71	21	0.0169	0.0169	4.0000	8.8300	0.0790	0.0640
Forum 12	119	169	71	21	0.0119	0.0000	2.8403	2.0000	0.0247	0.0040
Average SW	119	238	0	0	0.0336	0.0339	4.0000	7.6500	0.0874	0.0744
Forum 13	293	481	240	136	0.0056	0.0000	3.2833	3.0000	0.0112	0.0007
Average SW	293	586	0	0	0.0137	0.0137	4.0000	9.2300	0.0764	0.0617

Table 5.5 Directed preferential attachment random networks (the averages are for 100 random networks generated for each forum)

	Number of vertices	Number of lines	Loops	Multiple lines	Density 1	Density 2	Average degree	Diameter	Watts–Strogatz clustering coefficient	Network clustering coefficient (transitivity)
Forum 1	81	104	55	7	0.0159	0.0000	2.5679	2.0000	0.0000	0.0000
Average PA	81	159	0	24	0.0243	0.0246	3.9338	7.6082	0.1589	0.1460
Forum 2	160	333	126	36	0.0130	0.0000	4.1625	3.0000	0.0773	0.0079
Average PA	160	657	0	103	0.0257	0.0258	8.2094	7.5149	0.1491	0.1532
Forum 3	7	7	6	0	0.1429	0.0000	2.0000	1.0000	0.0000	0.0000
Average PA	7	11	0	4	0.2327	0.2714	3.2571	2.5941	0.3734	0.2872
Forum 4	170	658	345	328	0.0228	0.0000	7.7412	5.0000	0.4379	0.1333
Average PA	170	1275	0	255	0.0441	0.0444	15.4971	6.9300	0.1867	0.1944
Forum 5	88	93	86	9	0.0120	0.0000	2.1136	1.0000	0.0000	0.0000
Average PA	88	184	0	29	0.0237	0.0240	4.1793	7.6600	0.1635	0.1469
Forum 6	416	342	47	8	0.0020	0.0000	1.6442	4.0000	0.0392	0.0014
Average PA	416	708	0	54	0.0041	0.0883	3.4055	10.2800	0.0749	0.0883
Forum 7	157	375	202	147	0.0152	0.0000	4.7771	7.0000	0.0409	0.0245
Average PA	157	746	0	124	0.0303	0.0305	9.5010	7.4800	0.1613	0.1726
Forum 8	463	1219	748	591	0.0057	0.0000	5.2657	3.0000	0.0029	0.0014
Average PA	463	2436	0	258	0.0114	0.0114	10.5234	8.6200	0.0923	0.1102
Forum 9	650	1076	312	28	0.0025	0.0000	3.3108	8.0000	0.0253	0.0093
Average PA	650	2164	0	158	0.0051	0.0051	6.6573	10.2200	0.0633	0.0790
Forum 10	66	178	118	95	0.0409	0.0000	5.3939	2.0000	0.0422	0.0089
Average PA	66	344	0	79	0.0790	0.0802	10.4288	6.3000	0.2628	0.2681
Forum 11	237	573	96	141	0.0102	0.0000	4.8354	5.0000	0.1361	0.0241

(continued)

Table 5.5 (continued)

	Number of vertices	Number of lines	Loops	Multiple lines	Density 1	Density 2	Average degree	Diameter	Watts–Strogatz clustering coefficient	Network clustering coefficient (transitivity)
Average PA	237	1138	0	158	0.0203	0.0203	9.6009	7.9100	0.1307	0.1460
Forum 12	119	169	71	21	0.0119	0.0000	2.8403	2.0000	0.0247	0.0040
Average PA	119	351	0	54	0.0248	0.0250	5.9008	7.6900	0.1703	0.1826
Forum 13	293	481	240	136	0.0056	0.0000	3.2833	3.0000	0.0112	0.0007
Average PA	293	966	0	105	0.0112	0.0113	6.5937	8.9800	0.1036	0.1174

research is needed to determine the nature of these processes. The sparse nature of these networks may be due to a large proportion of deviant exchanges that are not visible to the researchers. This finding suggests they may be resilient to external disruption. The removal of one individual will not affect others because of the redundancy of services and user knowledge. These forums may also not be efficient as individuals must find ways to determine who is a legitimate seller or poster and minimize the risk of being ripped off. This finding provides further support for the presence of multiple markets that vary in structure and insularity from outsiders (see Herley & Florencio, 2010; Wehinger, 2011).

Summary

The visualizations and basic network characteristics presented here indicate that stolen data networks are generally inefficient, as they are neither dense nor well connected. This leads to frequent recycling of already existing information. These conditions may actually make the networks more challenging to disrupt, as they have a greater potential to be robust and rebound from any threat to their integrity (Bakker et al., 2012). The redundancy of sellers and buyers mean that the removal of one key actor may be replaced by another, making them more resistant to external disruption, unlike traditional hierarchical structures.

The most central users across most of these networks were sellers, though in some cases buyers and neutral players were almost equal in terms of network centrality. This is sensible given that sellers drive the market and engender the creation of threads within most of these forums (e.g. Motoyama et al., 2011). Buyers and neutral users create more posts than sellers, making them an integral part of network formation as they enable the flow of information and development of seller reputations over time. They most likely provide useful (or harmful) comments that may influence how other forum participants may interact with certain sellers.

Besides looking at global and local network characteristics that vary by the forum, we ran Monte Carlo simulations for the three major classes of random network models. Each of the random networks has its own hypotheses about how they can be generated. For example, in the preferential attachment models, the buyers and sellers would select forums where other buyers and sellers (or known to them actors) already participate. None of the random models can replicate fully the parameters of all our forums. However, the preferential attachment models closely reflect our real network models. This may signal a hybrid nature of hacker forums where random and systematic elements create stolen data markets. Thus, there is a need to take these elements into account when considering how to disrupt these markets most efficiently, whether through law enforcement interventions or other means.

Notes

1. For each model, the average and standard deviation of 100 random models were calculated which allows to run one-sample z-tests to identify whether our network measures fall within the range of random networks measures. This assumes that the parameters for 100 generated networks will follow a normal distribution.
2. The z-score is calculated according to the formula: raw score-mean divided by the standard deviation. Roughly, 95% of the data lies between ±3 standard deviations.

References

Adamic, L. A., & Glance, N. (2005, August). *The political blogosphere and the 2004 US election*: divided they blog. In Proceedings of the 3rd international workshop on Link discovery (pp. 36–43). ACM.

Bakker, R. M., Raab, J., & Milward, H. B. (2012). A preliminary theory of network resilience. *Journal of Policy Analysis and Management, 31*, 33–62.

Best, J., & Luckenbill, D. F. (1994). *Organizing deviance* (2nd ed.). New Jersey: Prentice Hall.

de Nooy, W., Mrvar, A., & Batagelj, V. (2005). *Exploratory social network analysis with Pajek*. Cambridge: Cambridge University Press.

Décary-Hétu, D., & Dupont, B. (2012). The social network of hackers. *Global Crime, 13*, 160–175.

Décary-Hétu, D., & Morselli, C. (2011). Gang presence in social network sites. *International Journal of Cyber Criminology, 5*(2), 876.

Granovetter, M. (1973). The strength of weak ties. *American Journal of Sociology, 78*, 1360–1380.

Herley, C., & Florencio, D. (2010). Nobody sells gold for the price of silver: Dishonesty, uncertainty and the underground economy. In T. Moor, D. J. Pym, & C. Ioannidis (Eds.), *Economics of information security and privacy* (pp. 35–53). New York: Springer.

Herring, S. C. (2004). Slouching toward the ordinary: Current trends in computer-mediated communication. *New Media & Society, 6*(1), 26–36.

Holt, T. J. (2007). Subcultural evolution? Examining the influence of on- and off-line experiences on deviant subcultures. *Deviant Behavior, 28*, 171–198.

Holt, T. J. (2009). Lone hacks or group cracks: Examining the social organization of computer hackers. In F. Smalleger & M. Pittaro (Eds.), *Crimes of the Internet* (pp. 336–355). Upper Saddle River, NJ: Pearson Prentice Hall.

Holt, T. J. (2010). Exploring strategies for qualitative criminological and criminal justice inquiry using on-line data. *Journal of Criminal Justice Education, 21*, 300–321.

Holt, T. J. (2013). Exploring the social organization and structure of stolen data markets. *Global Crime, 14*, 155–174.

Holt, T. J., & Blevins, K. R. (2007). Examining sex work from the client's perspective: Assessing johns using online data. *Deviant Behavior, 28*, 333–354.

Holt, T. J., Strumsky, D., Smirnova, O., & Kilger, M. (2012). Examining the social networks of malware writers and hackers. *International Journal of Cyber Criminology, 6*, 891–903.

Morselli, C., & Décary-Hétu, D. (2010). Crime facilitation purposes of social networking sites: A review and analysis of the "cyberbanging" phenomenon. *Small Wars & Insurgencies, 23*, 39–50.

Motoyama, M., McCoy, D., Levchenko, K., Savage, S., & Voelker, G. M. (2011). An analysis of underground forums. *IMC'11*, 71–79.

Robinson, M. (1984). *Groups*. New York: John Wiley & Sons.

Wasserman, S., & Faust, K. (1994). Social network analysis: Methods and applications (Vol. 8). Cambridge University Press.

Wehinger, F. (2011). The Dark Net: Self-regulation dynamics of illegal online markets for identities and related services. *Intelligence and Security Informatics Conference*, 209–213.

Womer, S., & Bunker, R. J. (2010). Sureños gangs and Mexican cartel use of social networking sites. *Small Wars & Insurgencies, 21*(1), 81–94.

Yip, M., Webber, C., & Shadbolt, N. (2013). Trust among cybercriminals? Carding forums, uncertainty, and implications for policing. *Policing and Society, 23*, 1–24.

Zhang, J., Ackerman, M. S., & Adamic, L. (2007). Expertise networks in online communities: Structure and algorithms. *WWW'07: Proceedings of the 16th International Conference on World Wide Web*, 221–230.

CHAPTER 6

Implications and Conclusions

Abstract This chapter provides a summary of all findings along with the implications for our understanding of illicit markets operating on- and offline. The stolen data markets examined here are similar in many respects to the other markets, such as those for stolen goods or drugs. There is one key difference that the nature of market precludes the buyers from inspecting the products and/or punishing sellers for non-working data. The policies to address the stolen data markets include collaboration between various law enforcement entities across jurisdictional lines, improved awareness of identity theft risks, and improvements in the reporting mechanisms for this form of criminality. Finally, there are certain limitations to this study, including that this is a snapshot of a selected number of forums at a given point in time. Future research will need to expand our understanding of how the stolen data markets evolve over time.

Keywords Legislation • Law enforcement • Market disruption • Chip and pin • Data theft

Throughout this work, we have identified the substantial threat that online forums where data thieves and cybercriminals can buy and sell information pose to consumers and corporations around the world (Holt & Lampke, 2010). The emergence of these forums provides actors with an open criminal marketplace where virtually any service or need can be acquired to engage in financially driven cybercrimes. These forums serve as a transformative resource for cybercrime, as individuals need not have any skill or capability to engage in cybercrime. Instead, they simply need to gain access to the market and identify a legitimate seller.

The stolen data marketplace constantly changes and evolves over time. There is a certain random component to the formation of the stolen data networks, but there are also certain consistent mechanisms that allow some forums to become more efficient vehicles of crimes. Our work has shown so far that nearly any type of data can be stolen and sold on these networks. The prices for the products vary greatly by the product type and forum type. The open comments serve as additional information about buyers and sellers on the forum that can enhance or hinder trust among the participants. The network structure is not efficient as a lot of old information is recycled, but resilient.

This chapter will provide an overview of the findings of this work, and their implications for our understanding of illicit markets operating on- and off-line. We will also explore future research questions that must be addressed in order to enhance our knowledge of data markets and their practices. We also consider how law enforcement agencies and policymakers may improve their response to the individuals who participate in stolen data markets and their operation as a whole. Finally, we explore future research questions that must be addressed in order to enhance our knowledge of data markets and their practices.

Market Economics

The forums themselves provide an open advertising platform whereby sellers create threads explaining their products, the price for information or services, their payment preferences, and contact details. In this respect, data markets are similar to real-world hawking markets for stolen goods (Cromwell, Olson, & Avary, 1993; Wright & Decker, 1994) or red light district strolls for sex work (Holzman & Pines, 1982; Scott & Dedel, 2006), as well as on-line markets for narcotics (Martin, 2014). Sellers offer their wares, but buyers have the ability to select the vendor they will work with.

Interested buyers then contacted the sellers outside of the forums, primarily through ICQ to negotiate the terms of their purchase. Payments were primarily sent through electronic payment systems such as WebMoney or Liberty Reserve, though a small proportion also accepted real-world payments through Western Union and MoneyGram (Franklin, Paxson, Perrig, & Savage, 2007; Holt & Lampke, 2010; Wehinger, 2011). After the purchase is completed, buyers could post a review of their experience with the seller so that others could see their feedback. Public comments enabled prospective buyers to research a vendor and gain some insights into the reputability of their claims. This is a key difference between real and virtual markets, since buyers can physically inspect a product or service provider in real-world illicit markets to determine their legitimacy. Since this is not possible in on-line markets, feedback serves as a valuable vetting tool to validate actor reputations and products.

In addition, the most common products sold in this sample of forums were various forms of illegally acquired personal data, though dumps and CVVs were the top two categories overall (see also Franklin et al., 2007; Holt & Lampke, 2010; Honeynet Research Alliance, 2003; Motoyama, McCoy, Levchenko, Savage, & Voelker, 2011). The advertised prices for data also varied greatly, with substantive differences based on the data's country of origin, suggesting that the quantity of available data acquired through breaches or phishing scams affected its price in the open market (see also Franklin et al., 2007; Herley & Florencio, 2010; Holt & Lampke, 2010).

There were, however, substantive variations in the types of products sold based on the nature of the forum itself. Two of the forums in this sample had a large number of complaints against sellers because they either accepted payment and sent no product or gave the buyer inactive or incomplete data. Comparing the distribution of products in the markets based on complaints of ripping suggests these unreliable forums sold a much larger percentage of data that could be fraudulently advertised. In fact, excluding ripping forums from the sample reduced the number of advertisements for dumps by half, and almost completely eliminated CVV ads.

This finding demonstrates that buyers face differentially greater risks of informal harm from their participation in stolen data markets relative to other illicit markets. There are no formal dispute resolution services that a buyer can employ in the event that they are cheated or ripped off by an untrustworthy vendor. The only recompense buyers have is to write bad reviews and call the seller a ripper in order to identify untrustworthy vendors and reduce others' risk of loss (see Franklin et al., 2007; Herley & Florencio, 2010; Holt & Lampke, 2010). Stolen data markets are, therefore, an ideal environment to cheat others in a similar fashion to robbing drug dealers in the real world (Cross, 2000; Jacobs, 1996, 2000; Jacobs, Topalli, & Wright, 2000).

The preponderance of ripping complaints in the English-language forums in this sample also demonstrates that stolen data markets are flooded with misinformation that buyers cannot easily interpret. This is surprising given the differences in virtual and real markets. For instance, actors in real-world markets must rely on hearsay and peers' knowledge in order to select a vendor or service provider, and have limited vendor choices due to geography and market size (Holzman & Pines, 1982; Jacobs, 1996; Wright & Decker, 1994). Buyers in virtual markets, however, should be much better informed consumers because they have the ability to review sellers' information before selecting a vendor and engaging in a transaction. The open, archival nature of forums enables buyers with the opportunity to read all advertisements and vendor feedback, thereby creating a more informed decision-making calculus for buyers. Despite the preponderance of information, buyers face great risks depending on which market they are able to access.

The findings presented in Chap. 3 demonstrate that there are multiple markets operating in order to sell data, though identifying the signals that demonstrate whether a market is reputable are not immediately apparent. Buyers can only observe what is posted publicly in the forums or perhaps what can be gleaned through off-forum conversation with the seller or other buyers. Feedback may be falsified, and the true quality of data can only be determined by making a purchase. Regression analyses demonstrated that there may be some prospective indicators of trust based on the price of data and the nature of the forum itself. One key predictor was the language used by participants supporting the assertion that Russian-language markets are more robust and trustworthy than those in other language formats (e.g. Symantec, 2014).

This finding is sensible given that US law enforcement agencies have attempted to disrupt English-language carding groups in a variety of ways over the last decade (Peretti, 2009; Poulsen, 2012). This may differentially increase the risk of participating in these communities as a legitimate vendor, as they may be subject to investigation and arrest. Instead, rippers may populate introductory-level English-language communities as they can easily operate with no risk and ensnare unfamiliar buyers with promises of low prices for valuable data. More experienced actors may attempt to enter and engage in Russian-language markets in order to obtain functional data and services while enhancing their risk of detection from law enforcement agencies in the USA which do not have the capability to examine these forums on a daily basis.

The economic analyses presented in Chap. 3 support this position, as disreputable markets may have lower general pricing in order to attract inexperienced buyers to make a purchase (Herley & Florencio, 2010; Wehinger, 2011). There were fewer successful transactions for data buyers observed in ripping markets relative to those in more insulated trustworthy markets. More insulated markets may have somewhat higher costs, though there is a lower risk of losing money and a greater degree of trust between participants (Herley & Florencio, 2010; Wehinger, 2011). As such, buyers can engage in transactions with greater ease and acquire what they need without difficulty.

The preliminary economic models presented also demonstrate that data sellers were able to earn thousands, if not millions, of dollars based on the observed feedback posted in these forums. Data buyers' returns were similarly variable, though it would appear that their profits could be substantially greater than those of data sellers (Herley & Florencio, 2010). Comparing the profits for buyers and sellers highlights an important relationship to real-world illicit markets. Specifically, data sellers received a small portion of the true value of the data that they offered, which is similar to research indicating that stolen goods vendors generate profits between 25 and 40 % of the actual value of the product (see also Schneider, 2005; Stevenson, Forsythe, & Weatherburn, 2001). Also, research on burglary and stolen goods markets suggests that offenders target products that consumers desire and seek to purchase through legitimate markets (Schneider, 2005; Stevenson et al., 2001; Wright & Decker, 1994). The amount of data acquired through breaches and phishing attacks suggests that data sellers may be attempting to satisfy demand from interested individuals in the broader cybercrime marketplace.

The findings point to a broader question that must be addressed in future research: what drives individuals to these markets and to take on specific roles. There is minimal research on the number of individuals who act as sellers within these markets who not only sell information but also use it for financial gain. Individuals who steal credit and debit cards no doubt realize the value of the information they acquire, though it is unclear why they choose to sell the information rather than use it to engage in fraud and theft. It may be that some cybercriminals perceive there to be less risk in simply stealing information and reselling it rather than using it for fraudulent transactions (Peretti, 2009). Alternatively, they may collect so much data that it is too time consuming to process for their own use, and instead accept smaller profits for the sake of quickly accepting payment for their services.

Research utilizing a rational choice framework to interview data thieves and participants in stolen data markets could be invaluable to improve our understanding of the decision-making processes of cybercriminals. Such research could also improve our knowledge of the career paths and process of becoming a data thief generally (e.g. Hutchings & Holt, 2015).

Considering the Social Organization of Data Markets

In addition to the economic conditions present in the market, this study also explored the organizational structure of participants in these forums. The findings indicate that the participants in stolen data forums operate at various stages of deviant sophistication. Those who sell and buy data appear to operate as colleagues within the market to facilitate the exchange of data. Individuals do not have to work with others, but the collegial environment provides access to those who can facilitate partnerships to achieve a specific goal (Franklin et al., 2007; Holt & Lampke, 2010; Motoyama et al., 2011). An individual could buy cards from one seller, and then seek out an encasher or provider who will liquidate an account. They may use these sellers again, or seek out others based on the availability of products and access to resources. Thus, the forums foster a substantive division of labor between participants based on the range of products and services available (Franklin et al., 2007; Herley & Florencio, 2010; Holt & Lampke, 2010; Motoyama et al., 2011; Wehinger, 2011).

At the same time, the buying and selling process is peer-driven since actors can engage one another and influence action through recommendations posted in a thread. Buyers can discuss their experiences and interactions with sellers, and those who receive extremely positive feedback may be more likely to gain multiple clients over time (Holt & Lampke, 2010; Motoyama et al., 2011). Forum administrators can provide reviews of products or influence the status of a seller, which may also affect their share of the market. Additionally, administrators can ban users on the basis of fraudulent claims in order to moderate user activity. These mechanisms help to reduce the risk of loss for buyers, though the relatively low barriers to enter and participate in a forum allow unscrupulous vendors to take advantage of prospective buyers (Herley & Florencio, 2010; Holt & Lampke, 2010; Motoyama et al., 2011). Individuals may ignore clear warning signs based on personal interests or needs and lose money with no formal recourse for compensation.

This study also demonstrates that these forums vary in their organizational complexity based on extended duration over time and the presence of purposive relationships between groups. Eight of the forums sampled constitute formal organizations, while the others appear to be driven by teams due to their short duration and generally limited organizational complexity. Interestingly, one of the forums with an extended duration was also a ripping forum. This suggests less reliable forums may operate for as long as more trustworthy markets, and supports the assertion that multiple markets operate at any point in time (Herley & Florencio, 2010; Wehinger, 2011). Our findings also indicate that there may be different stolen data markets based on the language of the primary participants, such as Russian or English. The penetration of police in English-language forums may have shifted actors and trust to Russian-language forums. At the same time, Russian-language forums may be flooded with information, making it difficult to identify all legitimate sellers.

Taken as a whole, this study demonstrates that hacker social organization has changed in the past two decades to function in more sophisticated and complex ways. At the same time, this research illustrates several areas for future research, including the need to refine and further develop the Best and Luckenbill (1994) framework. Their continuum of organizational sophistication allowed for differentiation between forms of organization based on the peer relationships of actors, and the impact of organizational involvement on participants' ability to offend. However, not all facets of stolen data market organizations fit within Best and Luckenbill's (1994) ideal types. For example, the categorization of these markets are complicated by their two-population composition: forum posters and forum operators or moderators. Thus, research is needed to explore and refine and operationalize the concepts that structure Best and Luckenbill's (1994) classification scheme with particular emphasis on virtual relationships. Such clarification is critical to better understand the social relationships between deviants and criminals, especially in light of deviants' increased reliance on the Internet to share information and identify others that share their interests (see Adler & Adler, 2006; Holt, 2007; Holt, 2009; Jewkes & Sharpe, 2003).

Researchers should also continue to examine the structure of stolen data market operations with larger and more diverse samples from various markets. While there was some evidence of sophisticated formal organizations, there was limited detail on their leadership, rules, and operations. This was due in part to the sampling framework we employed in this study, and our focus on posts from market-oriented sub-forums rather than operational posts and policies. Developing a sample of threads from various sub-forums within a single forum and comparing forums whose participants communicate in different languages would improve our understanding of the nature of these groups, and the benefits provided by membership (see also Franklin et al., 2007; Yip, Webber, & Shadbolt, 2013). Such a broad strategy may clarify the importance of groups and formal organizations within this relatively collegial marketplace.

The social network analyses presented also support the findings of both the economic and qualitative organizational analysis. The visualizations and basic network characteristics suggest that the networks present between actors in the market are generally inefficient, as they are neither dense nor well connected. These conditions may actually make the networks more challenging to disrupt, as they have a greater potential to be robust and rebound from any threat to their integrity (Bakker, Raab, & Milward, 2012). The redundancy of sellers and buyers mean that the removal of one key actor may be replaced by another, making them more resistant to external disruption, unlike traditional hierarchical structures.

The most central users across most of these networks were sellers, though in some cases buyers and neutral players were almost equal in terms of centrality. This is sensible given that sellers drive the market and engender the creation of threads within most of these forums. Buyers and neutral users create more posts, making them an integral part of network formation as they enable the flow of information and development of seller reputations over time. Monte Carlo simulations of networks underscore their hybrid nature, in that there is a certain randomness in how users may register, find, and favor various forums. There are also systematic ways in which users engage each other in the forums. The networks are also very sparse, especially compared to the other on-line networks, which may indicate the enormous amount of hidden information not yet accessible to the researchers.

Taken as a whole, the exploratory findings of this analysis suggest that the participants in these markets are generally collegial in nature (Best & Luckenbill, 1994). The hidden network structures identified suggest that there is a great deal of redundancy within the market, reducing the efficient flow of information between participants (see also Decary-Hetu & Dupont, 2012; Holt, Strumsky, Smirnova, & Kilger, 2012). As such, researchers must continue to explore these networks to identify any changes in their resilience and efficiency and understand when and how they may transform into more complex organizational structures.

It is also necessary for policymakers and the research community to recognize that the participants in these forums do not appear to be organized in the same sense as traditional organized crime groups like the Italian mafia or Yakuza (see Abadinsky, 2012; Jamieson, 2000; US Department of Justice, 2008). The markets have a clear division of labor present and an interest in economic gain by leveraging weaknesses in international security protocols and systems. There is, however, no evidence that the participants attempt to engage in violent behavior or corruption in order to further their goals, nor do they have a specifically insulated leadership structure (US Department of Justice, 2008).

As a whole, the forums operate on a continuum of structure on the basis of managerial engagement to provide a space where individuals can complete transactions on a one-to-one basis. There was little evidence of a truly insular hierarchical management structure present within or across the various forums' administration. Administrators, moderators, and testers are present in certain forums but make a small number of posts and may not engage in micro-management of transactions. It is possible that the organizational behavior of participants may change over time to become more hierarchical and efficient. At present, the markets do not appear to be a form of organized cybercrime, but rather a network of international cybercriminals operating in a collegial fashion to further their individual goals. This may be a function of the nature of the sample, as these markets were more introductory and readily accessible than other forums and on-line communities operating to sell information and cybercrime services. Further research is needed to investigate hidden or invitation-only forums, as their more sophisticated operations may be more efficient mechanisms for deviant exchanges (see Holt & Smirnova, 2014; Martin, 2014; Yip et al., 2013).

IMPLICATIONS FOR POLICY AND PRACTICE

The analyses presented here demonstrate that the market for stolen data is robust, and may not be easily or immediately disrupted through traditional interventions that may be employed to affect other forms of illicit markets (Franklin et al., 2007; Holt & Lampke, 2010; Wehinger, 2011). Given the global scope of harm that may result from the activities of data markets, there is a need to find ways to efficiently disrupt the flow of information and the networks that undergird their operation. This is a challenge, and requires consideration of broad-ranging solutions, including legislative changes as well as innovative law enforcement techniques.

One key strategy that has been put forth by computer scientists to affect cybercrime markets involves attacking the social validation systems that legitimize vendors. Specifically, Franklin and associates (2007) argued that two forms of attacks could be used to affect trust between participants: Sybil attacks and Slander attacks. In Sybil attacks, false on-line identities are created within each forum and are used to create advertisements for products which will simply rip off buyers. Slander attacks involve using fake identities to flood threads with groundless complaints against sellers in order to increase the difficulty in identifying legitimate sellers.

Such strategies seem appropriate as they target the informal systems that participants use to manage trust, and require virtually no monetary investment in order to support over the long term (Franklin et al., 2007). The use of these attacks may produce a short-term benefit by sewing confusion among participants, though it would likely only affect disorganized markets (see also Herley & Florencio, 2010). More organized and regulated forums with observant administrators would be able to diffuse and disrupt slander attacks shortly after they begin. The range of informal validation mechanisms available in structured markets, including escrow agents and testing services, make them insulated from Sybil attacks. In much the same way, administrators who regularly monitor their forums could ban identities that attempt to disrupt the market with Slander attacks posting false information regarding sellers. The general resiliency of the network structures observed in these forums suggests that there may be no easy or immediate way to disrupt them through external shocks to participants like slander attacks.

Instead, there may be greater value in targeting key resources used by market actors, regardless of whether it is a lemon market or one that is more organized. In that respect, law enforcement agencies may benefit from targeting the various electronic currencies used within the forums to accept and process payments, including WebMoney and Liberty Reserve. These resources are clear enablers of the underground economy and would disrupt the practices of stolen data vendors and buyers across both disorganized and organized markets. By increasing the difficulty actors would have to complete transactions and be paid for their services, it may reduce the number of successful exchanges within the market for a period of time (see Newman & Clarke, 2003).

There is a historical precedent for this tactic, as the US PATRIOT Act made it a federal crime to operate a money transmitter service without a license in any state where it is required, which was extended to include electronic currencies and international businesses that allowed US citizens to create accounts (Peretti, 2009). US law enforcement prosecuted the payment service e-Gold on four charges of money laundering due in part to its popularity among cybercriminals, including child pornographers and data thieves (Holt & Lampke, 2010; Peretti, 2009; Surowiecki, 2013). Members of the carding group, the ShadowCrew, and other underground markets, used e-Gold to send and receive payments for stolen data and cybercrime services (Holt & Lampke, 2010; Peretti, 2009). The investigation and prosecution of the service operators led market actors to identify other payment systems so as to minimize attention from law enforcement. This disruption may have affected the flow of money between actors for a short period of time while alternative systems were identified.

Similarly, the payment processor Liberty Reserve was shut down and its operators prosecuted in the USA for its role in money laundering in May 2013 (Surowiecki, 2013). This was a popular payment mechanism used by actors within the forums sampled, so it is not clear how vendors have begun to change their practices after its closure. The use of this tactic is not, however, a panacea for market disruption, and will only slow the total number of transactions occurring in any given market for a period of time. Buyers and sellers will undoubtedly adapt to other payment systems in order to continue profiting from the sale and use of stolen information. Thus, research is needed to understand if open web hosted data markets have adapted to crypto-currencies like Bitcoin, which have become the payment of choice in on-line drug markets (Martin, 2014). They may instead continue using electronic payment systems such as WebMoney and Yandex, which were used in this sample. Historical research is also needed to chart the progression and adoption of new payment systems by vendors across multiple markets. In turn, this may improve our knowledge of the ways that offenders displace to other venues in order to continue to offend (see also Holt, Blevins, & Kuhns, 2008; Newman & Clarke, 2003).

In addition, a range of vendors were observed for each product or service offered within these markets, whether they were organized or disorganized. If an individual vendor is arrested or removed from the market, it is likely their market share would be absorbed by other vendors and does little to disrupt the larger market operations. Thus, there may be greater benefit in targeting as many vendors at once while simultaneously affecting the perceived confidence that buyers may be able to place in the markets themselves. As such, a key strategy may be to have law enforcement agents create undercover identities and gain the trust of administrators and site operators. In turn, they may be able to gain control of entire forums and eventually conduct stings to take out as many key players (both sellers and administrators) behind the forums as is possible (Poulsen, 2012).

Such a tactic may have substantive value, as federal agencies have infiltrated several forums through participation as data buyers, or in some cases, by turning market participants into confidential informants (Poulsen, 2012). Using these strategies could allow for the implementation of intelligence-led policing strategies to track the behavior of participants, identify key buyers and sellers, and build cases against entire networks of individuals (see also Poulsen, 2012). This technique was successfully employed by law enforcement during the "Dark Market" case where an undercover FBI agent was able to garner the trust of the forum operator. In fact, he became an administrator and actually began to host the forum on an undercover server so that law enforcement could obtain the IP addresses of individuals connecting to the site. The intensive investigative techniques led to over 60 arrests and prosecutions against the buyers and sellers involved in the site (Poulsen, 2012). Not only would such an investigative strategy ensure sufficient evidence against the participants, but also create confusion and mistrust between market actors. The resulting arrests would also affect both the supply and demand side of the market in ripping and non-ripping forums alike due to cascading concerns over reputation and legitimacy.

Beyond law enforcement strategies, there is a need for improved international cooperative agreements to facilitate the international investigation and prosecution of cybercriminals (see also Brenner, 2008). The findings of this study demonstrate that participants are compromising banks, businesses, and citizens primarily in the USA and EU. The forum participants may live anywhere, though the language preferences observed suggest some are native to the Russian Federation or are expatriates living abroad. The forums are also hosted on web servers residing around the world, with the potential to move to other services if they are compromised.

The international dynamics at play make it extremely difficult for any one nation to investigate and successfully prosecute an offender. The likelihood of successful prosecutions is limited by the fact that nations with large criminal hacker populations such as Russia and the Ukraine do not have an extradition relationship with the USA. Investigations can be undertaken, though it will be unlikely that a prosecution of a Russian national living in the country will be successful because they cannot be brought to the USA for trial. This issue has led some federal prosecutors to choose not to take on cases because of the perception that there will be no actual case to be made in court without the offender present. As a consequence, there are few ways to deter actors in these nations from targeting the USA and other countries in which no formal extradition treaties exist.

Instead, law enforcement agencies must network and find ways to collaborate during cases in order to bring cybercriminals to justice. One of the few critical successes employed by law enforcement is the use of working relationships between agencies in order to arrest individuals from Russia and Ukraine while they are traveling abroad to countries with a friendly extradition relationship to the USA. For instance, Aleksi Kolorov, a Bulgarian national, was initially indicted as part of the ShadowCrew bust in 2005 (see Chap. 1), but not arrested due to his residence in a country with ineffectual relations to support an extradition (Zetter, 2013). He was finally extradited to the USA in 2013 after being arrested in Paraguay in 2011 by their national police on unrelated fraud charges involving the misuse of credit and debit card data from Paraguayan banks. Once in custody, Kolorov was brought to the attention of US prosecutors who were able to successfully negotiate a transfer to the USA after two years of detention in Paraguay (Zetter, 2013). This is, however, an infrequent possibility that demands improved international intelligence collection and law enforcement cooperation in order to identify, arrest, and prosecute cybercriminals generally.

Since prosecutions are not always possible, there is also a need to ensure that the criminal law keeps pace with the scope of financial harm that can be caused by actors involved in data theft. The majority of federal criminal cases in the USA involve the use of the Computer Fraud and Abuse Act (CFAA), which criminalizes the misuse of computers, personal data, and passwords (Peretti, 2009). The use of wire fraud statutes may also be employed depending on the nature of the offense. These laws are effective in dealing with hacking cases, particularly the individuals who acquire data through phishing, data breaches, and malware.

If, however, an actor buys data from a vendor, and does not use a US computer system in order to acquire information then there are few legal mechanisms that can be employed to pursue criminal charges against that person. Thus, the Department of Justice has begun to lobby Congress to develop legislation that criminalizes the sale, purchase, or possession of credit/debit card information issued from a US bank, no matter where in the world a transaction takes place (Tucker, 2014). This would enable improved prosecutions of the data buyers who may engender so much of the market demand for stolen information.

Additionally, such legislation would enable prosecutors to seek enhanced sentences for offenders if they are caught. For instance, Vladislav Horohorin was a hacker with citizenship in Russia, Israel, and the Ukraine and participated in multiple underground forums as a data seller and hacker (Department of Justice, 2013). Horohorin had been indicted in 2009 and 2010 in the USA on charges under the CFAA, as well as wire fraud, conspiracy to commit wire fraud (Department of Justice, 2013) for hacking into various companies and payment processors. He was wanted for arrest, but was unable to be extradited until he was identified in Nice, France boarding a flight back to Moscow, Russia.

Law enforcement officers from both France and the US Secret Service arrested Horohorin in Nice and found he was in possession of 2.5 million stolen credit and debit card numbers (Department of Justice, 2013). There was no way to pursue further charges against him for possession of these materials, thus he was extradited to the USA in 2012 and prosecuted for his existing charges. He was found guilty on two counts of CFAA violations and conspiracy to commit wire fraud and sentenced to 88 months in prison and a fine of $125,739 (Department of Justice, 2013). Had there been a way to charge him for the possession of the stolen data found on his person, Horohorin may have received a more severe sentence befitting the scope of his crimes.

There is also a need for improved awareness of the risks of electronic identity theft among the general public who do not necessarily have a strong grasp of basic computer security principals (Holt & Lampke, 2010; James, 2005; Newman & Clarke, 2003; Wall, 2007). The number of mass data breaches in the USA over the last few years may have increased the recognition among consumers that they may lose their personal information through a compromise at a retailer or financial service provider. This has led to an emphasis on financial institutions reissuing credit and debit cards in the event a card may have been compromised. While this has the short-term benefit of invalidating that card for use, an individual's personal information may still be made available and sold on the market. Thus, there is a need for the implementation of other techniques to minimize the risk of data loss.

One key strategy that has been recently deployed across the USA in 2014 is the use of "Chip and Pin" or EMV (Europay, MasterCard, and Visa) technologies, which should protect consumers and increase the difficulty offenders have in capturing or manipulating stolen data. Financial institutions provide account holders with cards that have an integrated circuit or computer chip which authenticates a transaction at point-of-sale terminals and ATMs (Pavia, Veres-Ferrer, & Foix-Escura, 2012). These cards require that the users insert their card into a specially designed point-of-sale terminal when attempting to complete an in-store transaction that connects the chip on the card to the payment system. The account holder must then enter a PIN which authenticates the card, the chip, and the PIN through bank servers (Pavia et al., 2012). These technologies provide a greater degree of security for the account holder, as the magnetic strip data on the card may be captured through malware or other means, but not the actual integrated chip. As a result, fraudsters who acquire data from EMV or chip and pin cards are unable to use them to complete transactions in brick-and-mortar stores and point-of-sale terminals (Pavia et al., 2012; Sullivan, 2013; Wilson, 2012).

The adoption of chip and pin technologies first began in Europe and appear to have had a direct impact on fraud losses. When chip and pin technology was implemented across the UK in 2003, there was a direct and observable reduction in fraud losses in 2005, which has been associated with the increased difficulty offenders had in using stolen data in stores (Hayashi & Sullivan, 2013). There was, however, an observable increase in the number of on-line and phone-based purchases made using fraudulently obtained data to make purchases because different, weaker security protocols are in place in these transactions (Hayashi & Sullivan, 2013). This may account for the fact that individuals are still able to sell dumps from the UK and EU in these forums, as data can still be used to engage in fraud in different environments. This also represents one of the key adjustments or displacement practices offenders can use in stolen data market: as one venue for criminal activity closes, users displace their practices to another strategy in order to be effective (see Holt et al., 2008; Newman & Clarke, 2003).

Since the USA has experienced a massive increase in mega-breaches, and consumers have had minimal experience with chip and pin card technology, it is unclear how consumers will respond to this new system. In fact, there is no consistent implementation of this hardware and software at point-of-sale terminals, suggesting consumers are not yet forced to use this technology across all retailers. Researchers estimate we may see similar declines in fraud in the UK and France, though it will depend entirely on customer education and the ways that authorization and authentication protocols are implemented (e.g. Hayashi & Sullivan, 2013; Sullivan, 2013). There is a need for research considering how these technologies are being accepted by consumers and any recognition of the prospective value of these cards to minimize the threat of victimization.

Though attempts are being made to curb threats to organizational data loss, that does not reduce the likelihood of fraud victimization via other methods including responding to a phishing email (James, 2005), via malicious software infection on a PC (Holt & Turner, 2012), or even downloading a rogue banking application for a smartphone or tablet. There is no single way to reduce individual risk of harm; there is a need for public awareness campaigns to promote basic computer security principals and vigilance against identity theft. Consumers must be informed regularly of the threats that emerge from responding to unsolicited email, clicking on suspicious web links, and the need to run antivirus and security tools to help decrease their risk of victimization (Bossler & Holt, 2009; Holt & Turner, 2012). General education is also needed to promote the importance of regularly checking bank and credit card statements for suspect charges. Individuals also need to avoid making purchases through on-line vendors with no security features in place to protect personal information. Such information could be rolled out effectively through financial institutions, schools (particularly in middle and high school), as well as the Federal Trade Commission to promote general security and diminish the scope of the threat of on-line fraud.

There is also a need to dramatically improve our reporting systems for fraud and identity crimes enabled by technology. At present, there are few reporting sources that enable the public to recognize when and how fraud is taking place and the total amount of fraud losses experienced from different payment categories (Hayashi & Sullivan, 2013; Wilson, 2012). The FBI's Uniform Crime Report provides no information on high-tech identity theft, nor does the National Incident Based Reporting System (e.g. Holt & Bossler, 2016). The only real resource is the NCVS's special supplemental study on identity theft, which does not provide segmentation on the way individual identity theft was committed. As a result, there is a need for improved reporting of identity theft via law enforcement sources and financial institutions in order to improve transparency regarding the true number of individuals affected by data breaches and high-tech fraud, and to what degree in as timely a fashion as is possible in order to better track the scope of economic harm experienced year to year. This may require cooperation and coordination among state legislatures to appropriately develop laws mandating reporting of fraud. For example, in 2004, only California required businesses to report the stolen data information to their consumers, but by 2010, 46 states have such laws on their books (Holt, Bossler, & Seigfried-Spellar, 2015). Thus, the construction of consumer protection must be locally constructed in order to help combat the global effects of stolen data markets.

Limitations of the Current Study

Though this study provides initial insights into the nature and practices of stolen data markets, there is a need for further research using primary data collection to address the limitations of this work. Specifically, this analysis was based on data derived from open and registration-only forums, which may be different from that of closed and vetted membership forums that may be more insulated from outsiders. The data is also temporally bound, and only reflects the practices of this type of market during the mid-to-late 2000s. As a result, the findings may not be generalizable to more organized and hidden markets, or those that are currently in operation today.

It is imperative that future researchers find ways to access hidden and more sophisticated forums in order to improve our knowledge of the tiered structure of stolen data markets and the ways actors engage in the sale of information and services. This includes collecting data from forums and shops that may operate on the encrypted Tor markets used to sell narcotics and other services (Martin, 2014). For example, the economic estimates derived from this sample may be radically different from the number of transactions that may take place in more trustworthy markets. Models produced by data generated from open forums may not truly reflect the actual costs for data and the forces that affect participant behavior (Herley & Florencio, 2010). Developing data from open forums, closed by registration, and registration-only vetted communities is essential to better estimate the products sold and the prospective return on investments that buyers may receive across the total underground market for data. Similarly, collecting information on the number of contacts and transactions completed outside of the forum may directly affect the shape of social networks of forum participants, as well as the centrality of a user as can be observed in the forum posts alone. This may help to develop more targeted policies toward the stolen data markets disruptions.

Additionally, researchers should strive to find ways to access the private exchanges between participants in the markets in order to augment the information posted publicly in forums. For example, individuals may be able to negotiate the price for data or services down from the publicly posted prices a seller lists in their ads (Franklin et al., 2007; Holt & Lampke, 2010; Holz, Engelberth, & Freiling, 2009; Honeynet Research Alliance, 2003; Motoyama et al., 2011; Wehinger, 2011). There are only three possible ways to gather such data at present: (1) utilize data from closed forums that have been publicly archived on-line by researchers or hackers, (2) pose as an actor in a site and engage in covert transactions with prospective sellers, or (3) work with law enforcement agencies to obtain exchanges they have engaged in with underground actors.

The first option may provide unique insights, though the data are often limited in terms of their value to understand the current practices of the market (e.g. Yip et al., 2013). The second and third options are more challenging, as they pose ethical dilemmas for academic researchers (see Holt, 2010; Markham, 2011). It may not be possible for a researcher at an academic institution to engage in transactions without violating laws or tenets of ethical research because they are facilitating criminal activity (see Holt, 2010; Markham, 2011).

Law enforcement agencies may also be hesitant to provide information as it may compromise an investigation or the chain of evidence used in a prosecution. There are few alternatives to identify data of this nature in the wild, thus we encourage researchers to foster relationships with law enforcement in order to enhance the amount of information that may be available to understand the practices of data thieves. Such a relationship could prove mutually beneficial, as academic researchers could provide depth on the practices of communities at a strategic level that may not be possible for law enforcement agencies to cultivate over time.

Further research is also needed with larger longitudinal data sets to understand the way that forums change over time. While some of these forums in this sample operated over several years of time, the use of single sub-forums does not provide further context for actor or forum evolution as changes occurring in other parts of the site may directly affect operations in the forums sampled. For instance, we can determine an individual's participation in multiple threads in one forum, though there may be missing data involving encounters with other individuals in separate sections of the site. Capturing multiple sub-forums within a site and tracking users over time would allow for the development of complex network models of change and assessments of network centrality and density over time. In turn, this would allow for the identification of key points in the evolution of a forum from legitimate to ripping, or vice versa.

In addition, the majority of the networks explored here appear to be largely inefficient, but also resilient to external shocks. This structure may change over time, particularly as a consequence of researcher and law enforcement interventions that attempt to disrupt the markets (see Chu, Holt, & Ahn, 2010; Holt, 2010). Longitudinal research utilizing surreptitious data collection strategies in various forums could improve our knowledge of key points in the evolution of the market over time. In fact, this may enable researchers to identify if and when markets begin to transition from collegial structures to more organized and efficient marketplaces. Such information is vital to understand how markets become "lemons" and which become more legitimate in the underground. In turn, this information would greatly expand our knowledge of the nature of stolen data markets and their role in cybercrime and fraud globally.

References

Abadinsky, H. (2012). *Organized crime* (10th ed.). New York: Cengage Learning.

Adler, P. A., & Adler, P. (2006). Self-injurers as loners: The social organization of solitary deviance. *Deviant Behavior, 26*, 345–378.

Bakker, R. M., Raab, J., & Milward, H. B. (2012). A preliminary theory of network resilience. *Journal of Policy Analysis and Management, 31*, 33–62.

Best, J., & Luckenbill, D. F. (1994). *Organizing deviance* (2nd ed.). New Jersey: Prentice Hall.

Bossler, A. M., & Holt, T. J. (2009). On-line activities, guardianship, and malware infection: An examination of routine activities theory. *International Journal of Cyber Criminology, 3*, 400–420.

Brenner, S. W. (2008). *Cyberthreats: The emerging fault lines of the nation state.* New York: Oxford University Press.

Chu, B., Holt, T. J., & Ahn, G. J. (2010). *Examining the creation, distribution, and function of malware on-line.* Technical Report for National Institute of Justice. NIJ Grant No. 2007-IJ-CX-0018. Retrieved from http://www.ncjrs.gov/pdffiles1/nij/grants/230112.pdf

Cromwell, P. F., Olson, J. N., & Avary, D. W. (1993). Who buys stolen property? A new look at criminal receiving. *Journal of Crime and Justice, 16*, 75–95.

Cross, J. C. (2000). Passing the buck: Risk avoidance and risk management in the illegal/informal drug trade. *International Journal of Sociology and Social Policy, 20*, 68–94.

Decary-Hetu, D., & Dupont, B. (2012). The social network of hackers. *Global Crime, 13*, 160–175.

Franklin, J., Paxson, V., Perrig, A., & Savage, S. (2007). *An inquiry into the nature and cause of the wealth of internet miscreants.* Paper presented at CCS07, October 29–November 2, 2007, Alexandria, VA.

Hayashi, F., & Sullivan, R. J. (2013). Fees, fraud, and regulation: Forces of change in the payment card industry. *Payment Systems Research Briefing*. Federal Reserve Bank of Kansas City. Retrieved from https://www.kc.frb.org/publicat/psr/briefings/psr-briefingapr2013.pdf

Herley, C., & Florencio, D. (2010). Nobody sells gold for the price of silver: Dishonesty, uncertainty and the underground economy. In T. Moor, D. J. Pym, & C. Ioannidis (Eds.), *Economics of information security and privacy* (pp. 35–53). New York: Springer.

Holt, T. J. (2007). Subcultural evolution? Examining the influence of on- and offline experiences on deviant subcultures. *Deviant Behavior, 28*, 171–198.

Holt, T. J. (2009). Lone hacks or group cracks: Examining the social organization of computer hackers. In F. Smalleger & M. Pittaro (Eds.), *Crimes of the Internet* (pp. 336–355). Upper Saddle River, NJ: Pearson Prentice Hall.

Holt, T. J. (2010). Exploring strategies for qualitative criminological and criminal justice inquiry using on-line data. *Journal of Criminal Justice Education, 21*, 300–321.

Holt, T. J., & Turner, M. G. (2012). Examining risks and protective factors of on-line identity theft. *Deviant Behavior, 33*, 308–323.

Holt, T. J., & Lampke, E. (2010). Exploring stolen data markets on-line: Products and market forces. *Criminal Justice Studies, 23*, 33–50.

Holt, T. J., & Smirnova, O. (2014). *Examining the structure, organization, and processes of the international market for stolen data*. Washington, DC: US Department of Justice. Retrieved from https://www.ncjrs.gov/pdffiles1/nij/grants/245375.pdf

Holt, T. J., Blevins, K. R., & Kuhns, J. B. (2008). Examining the displacement practices of Johns with on-line data. *Journal of Criminal Justice, 36*, 522–528.

Holt, T. J., & Bossler, A. M. (2016). *Cybercrime in progress: Theory and prevention of technology-enabled offenses*. New York: Routledge Press.

Holt, T. J., Bossler, A. M., & Seigfried Spellar, K. C. (2015). Cybercrime and digital forensics: An introduction. New York: Routledge Press.

Holt, T. J., Strumsky, D., Smirnova, O., & Kilger, M. (2012). Examining the social networks of malware writers and hackers. *International Journal of Cyber Criminology, 6*, 891–903.

Holz, T., Engelberth, M., & Freiling, F. (2009). Learning more about the underground economy: A case-study of keyloggers and dropzones. In M. Backes & P. Ning (Eds.), *Computer security—ESCORICS* (pp. 1–18). Berlin and Heidelberg: Springer.

Holzman, H. R., & Pines, S. (1982). Buying sex: The phenomenology of being a John. *Deviant Behavior, 4*(1), 89–116.

Honeynet Research Alliance. (2003). Profile: Automated credit card fraud. *Know Your Enemy Paper* series. Retrieved from http://www.honeynet.org/papers/profiles/ccfraud.pdf

Hutchings, A., & Holt, T. J. (2015). A crime script analysis of the online stolen data market. *British Journal of Criminology, 55*(3), 596–614.
Jacobs, B. (1996). Crack dealers apprehension avoidance techniques: A case of restrictive deterrence. *Criminology, 34,* 409–431.
Jacobs, B. (2000). *Robbing drug dealers: Violence beyond the law.* New York: Aldine de Gruyter.
Jacobs, B. A., Topalli, V., & Wright, R. (2000). Managing retaliation: Drug robbery and informal sanction threats. *Criminology, 38,* 171–198.
James, L. (2005). *Phishing exposed.* Rockland, MA: Syngress.
Jamieson, A. (2000). *The antimafia: Italy's fight against organized crime.* New York: Palgrave Macmillian.
Jewkes, Y., & Sharp, K. (2003). Crime, deviance and the disembodied self: Transcending the dangers of corporeality. In Y. Jewkes (Ed.), *Dot.cons: Crime, deviance and identity on the Internet* (pp. 1–14). Portland, OR: Willan Publishing.
Markham, A. N. (2011). Internet research. In D. Silverman (Ed.), *Qualitative research: Issues of theory, method, and practice* (3rd ed., pp. 111–127). Thousand Oaks, CA: Sage.
Martin, J. (2014). Lost on the Silk Road: Online drug distribution and the cryptomarket. *Criminology and Criminal Justice, 14,* 351–367.
Motoyama, M., McCoy, D., Levchenko, K., Savage, S., & Voelker, G. M. (2011). An analysis of underground forums. *IMC'11,* 71–79.
Newman, G., & Clarke, R. (2003). *Superhighway robbery: Preventing e-commerce crime.* Cullompton: Willan Press.
Pavia, J. M., Veres-Ferrer, E. J., & Foix-Escura, G. (2012). Credit card incidents and control systems. *International Journal of Information Management, 32,* 501–503.
Peretti, K. K. (2009). Data breaches: What the underground world of "carding" reveals. *Santa Clara Computer and High Technology Law Journal, 25,* 375–413.
Poulsen, K. (2012). *Kingpin: How one hacker took over the billion dollar cybercrime underground.* New York: Broadway.
Scott, M. S., & Dedel, K. (2006). *Street prostitution.* US Department of Justice, Office of Community Oriented Policing Services.
Schneider, J. L. (2005). Stolen-goods markets: Methods of disposal. *British Journal of Criminology, 45,* 129–140.
Stevenson, R. J., Forsythe, L. M. V., & Weatherburn, D. (2001). The stolen goods market in New South Wales Australia: An analysis of disposal avenues and tactics. *British Journal of Criminology, 41,* 101–118.
Sullivan, R. J. (2013). The US adoption of computer-chip payment cards: Implications for payment fraud. *Economic Review.* Federal Reserve Bank of Kansas City.

Surowiecki, J. (2013). Why did criminals trust liberty reserve. *The New Yorker*, May 31. Retrieved from http://www.newyorker.com/online/blogs/newsdesk/2013/05/why-did-criminals-trust- liberty-reserve.html

Symantec Corporation. (2014). *Symantec Internet security threat report*, Volume 19. http://www.symantec.com/threatreport/.

Tucker, E. (2014). One simple legal fix could help fight overseas credit card fraud, claims DOJ. *PBS Newshour*. Retrieved from http://www.pbs.org/newshour/rundown/one-simple-legal-fix-help-justice-department-fight-overseas-credit-card-fraud/

U.S. Department of Justice. (2008). *Overview of the law enforcement strategy to combat international organized crime*. Washington, DC: U.S. Department of Justice. Retrieved from http://www.justice.gov/ag/speeches/2008/ioc-strategy-public-overview.pdf

U.S. Department of Justice. (2013). *International credit card trafficker sentenced to 88 months in prison*. Washington, DC: Department of Justice Office of Public Affairs. Retrieved from http://www.justice.gov/opa/pr/international-credit-card-trafficker-sentenced-88-months-prison

Wall, D. S. (2007). *Cybercrime: The transformation of crime in the information age*. Cambridge: Polity Press.

Wehinger, F. (2011). The Dark Net: Self-regulation dynamics of illegal online markets for identities and related services. *Intelligence and Security Informatics Conference*, 209–213.

Wilson, S. (2012). Calling for a uniform approach to card fraud offline and on. *Journal of Internet Banking and Commerce, 17*, 1–5.

Wright, R. T., & Decker, S. H. (1994). *Burglars on the job: Streetlife and residential break-ins*. Boston, MA: Northeastern University Press.

Yip, M., Webber, C., & Shadbolt, N. (2013). Trust among cybercriminals? Carding forums, uncertainty, and implications for policing. *Policing and Society, 23*, 1–24.

Zetter, K. (2013). 9 years after Shadowcrew, Feds get their hands on fugitive cybercrook. *Wired*, July 1. Retrieved from http://www.wired.com/2013/07/bulgarian-shadowcrew-arrest/

Index

A
administrator, forum, 5, 84, 86, 87, 89, 93, 138
arc, 100

C
carding, defined, 10–11, 55, 136
chip and pin, 146–7
colleagues, 75, 76, 99
Computer Fraud and Abuse Act, 145
credit verification value (CVV), 1, 21, 26, 37, 39, 41, 65, 67, 70, 83, 135
　cost of, 7, 36
　profit from, 63–9
customer service, 32–3, 41, 49–51, 53
cybercrime, defined, 4, 6, 8, 13, 24, 46–9, 82, 141–3

D
data breach, 2–3, 38, 46–7, 62, 83, 146
drops service, 4, 82, 83

dump, 2–5, 32–4, 36–7, 52–5, 59–61
　availability by country, 25, 39–41, 135
　factors affecting, 49, 55
　price, 25, 26, 37, 39, 41, 45, 46, 49, 53–5, 63
　profits from, 58, 63, 67–8

E
e-Bay (eBay) accounts, 22, 26, 37, 46, 49–53, 55, 58–61, 63, 66–7, 70
e-Gold, 3, 13, 143
email addresses, 20, 29
encashment, 22, 78

F
feedback
　negative, 5, 34, 41–2, 46, 52, 56–9, 69, 80–1, 93
　positive, 5, 35, 42, 46, 52, 53, 55–9, 61, 67, 69, 79, 80, 93, 138
　role of feedback, 5, 34, 52, 60, 79, 80, 135, 136

156 INDEX

forum, defined, 3–7, 9–15, 19–22, 25, 26, 28, 30, 32–42, 45–55, 58–70, 73–93, 97–100, 102–30, 133–44, 149–51

H
hacking, 13, 145–6
hijacking, 38, 52, 55

I
ICQ, 3, 28–9, 32, 50, 104, 134
identity theft, 4, 8, 61–2, 67–8, 133, 146, 148

J
J-curve, 9, 117–18, 125

L
lemon market, lemonizing, 45, 48–53, 55, 58, 63, 67, 69–70, 142
liberty reserve, 13, 30, 50, 53–5, 142, 143
logs, 81, 89

M
malware (malicious software), 6, 26–7, 36, 37, 86, 147
moderator, forum, 33, 51, 84, 86, 90
Monte Carlo Simulations, 97, 122, 125, 129, 140
mules, 23–4
mutual association, 73, 75–6, 78–82
mutual participation, 78–82

N
network disruption
  resilience, 129
  robustness, 4, 22, 99, 129, 136, 140, 141
network measures
  centrality, 103–5, 109–20, 129
  component/giant component, 103, 108–9, 111–22
  degree, 106–9, 122–8
  density, 102–3, 106–7, 123, 124, 126–8, 150

O
organized crime, 141

P
paypal accounts, 20, 26, 31, 37, 46, 50, 58, 63, 67
peers, 73, 75, 76, 79, 83, 92, 136
phishing, 28, 135, 137, 145, 148
plastics, 21, 27, 36, 37
product testing, 33, 84, 85, 87, 93

R
random networks, 120, 122, 123, 125–7, 129
reputation, 5, 48, 51–2, 79, 80, 82–4, 88, 93, 104, 108, 109, 117, 129, 135, 140, 144
ripper, 34–7, 48–9, 53, 55–6, 67, 78, 87–8, 135–6
Russian (language), 1, 8–9, 11–12, 36, 37, 39, 53, 55, 136, 139

S
Shadowcrew, bust, 143, 145
social network analysis, 97–105
  resiliency, 99
social organization
  Best and Luckenbill model, 14, 73–8
spam, 21, 24, 26–7, 36–7

T
teams, 75–6, 83, 93, 99, 139

V
validated seller, 6, 32, 47, 51, 56, 98, 135, 142, 146
vertex, 104

W
WebMoney, 50, 53–5, 78, 134, 142–3
Western Union, 3, 30, 50, 53–5

The manufacturer's authorised representative in the EU is Springer Nature Customer Service Centre GmbH, Europaplatz 3, 69115 Heidelberg, Germany. If you have any concerns regarding our products, please contact ProductSafety@springernature.com

Printed and bound by CPI Group (UK) Ltd, Croydon, CR0 4YY

23/03/2026

02076402-0008